SHAPED

A Biography

by

Barbara Umuhoza

ÉCLAT PUBLISHING

Kigali, Rwanda

www.eclatpublishing.com

Cover & Layout: Ibrahim A. Hassan
Editors: Gael Rutembesa & Oscar Kimanuka
Cover Photo: Sabin Abayo

We hope you enjoy this book from Éclat Publishing.
Our mission is to provide high-quality, life transforming books and products that connect you to truth, restore hope and empower your life.
For more information on other books and products written and produced; please contact Éclat Publishing;

ISBN Softcover: 978-99977-0-351-4

ÉCLAT PUBLISHING
KG 24. Kigali - Rwanda.
Email: info@eclatpublishing.com

Printed in EA

To Abba Father,

Thank you for knowing, loving and shaping me before I was a seed in my mother's womb.

To my Parents;

Mpfizi Barnabé and Kantengwa Laurette who believed in me and showed me that I could become anything that I ever dreamt of.

To my Two Sons;

Koen R. and Keshawn R. Habumugisha whose constant love is the spice of my life.

To my Shapers in and beyond this book;
You have made each life moment count for the best.

Contents

FOREWORD

I first met Barbara in December 2010 when she and her father, Papa Barnabe Mpfizi, who is my first cousin, came to Dar es Salaam to attend my eldest daughter, Rebecca's wedding send-off ceremony. Barbara played a key role in injecting the Rwandan style, flair and tradition in the ceremony. She was the stylist and dance director of the event and from the word go, I loved her enthusiasm and passion. By the time of our first meeting, unbeknown to me then, Barbara, already had had experiences of a lifetime.

I next met Barbara at her own wedding in July 2011 in Kigali. It was a bitter-sweet moment because while we celebrated her matrimonial vows, her mother Laurette, (La charmante) as I used to call her, lay wasting away from a terminal disease, unable to join in the festivities. The sad backdrop to the wedding did not dampen our enthusiasm- after all I had travelled, along with my wife Margaret, all the way from Mbabane- where I was serving as the United Nations Representative and Resident Coordinator of the United Nations System in Swaziland, to attend. We all knew that Laurette was with us in spirit and would have wished nothing but happiness for her beloved daughter on such an auspicious occasion.

When Barbara asked me to write a foreword for her book, "SHAPED" I did not hesitate to ask why me? Yet, I found it an honor for my niece to associate me with her work. In accepting, even before reading the book, I also found it inspiring that unlike the rest of us, Barbara had the discipline to sit down and write publishable material. Along with internalizing the messages of this book, we all should emulate her and take the challenge to put pen to paper and publish.

SHAPED is a short journey through Barbara's life. Yet it carries lessons of a lifetime. From her recollection of a modest but loving early life in Burundi, and in Kampala, Uganda, Barbara recounts her joy of childhood, her longing to return to the "promised" land-Rwanda, a place she could only conjure in her imagination stroked by stories of patriotism, bravery and sacrifice of the "Inkotanyi', of song and dance that her "social butterfly" mother taught her. Soon those beautiful images were to be replaced by apprehensions and fear as the genocide against the Tutsi unfolded and tragedy struck home with the loss of uncle Rutayisire.

Moving to a post genocide Rwanda after surviving the uncertainties of exile and starting from afresh building a new life at HOME, making new friends and adjusting to new socio-political circumstances, were among the early experiences that build Barbara's, character and fortitude in her approach to life from early on.

The few years in England were pivotal as Barbara, a teenager was thrust in the middle of the boxing ring of life without the necessary skills and tools. Yet she battles through, connecting with family and friends, building strong church fellowship networks, juggling the daily hustle with college and working the Government system to obtain a UK residence permit. The Damascene moment at the Hatton Cross Tribunal Centre that she recounts in the book, is one of her experiences, which I find most compelling. To the amazement of the British Government Solicitor, and admiration of the Presiding Judge, Barbara decided to tell the truth about her motivation applying for asylum and voluntarily ended the process. She chose to return to Rwanda. By that heroic personal act, Barbara had conquered the untruth and liberated her soul. How could she be the person of faith and prayer, yet live a life that was not completely true? She had sacrificed, not in vain. She understood that sacrifice will always be rewarded.

Returning to Rwanda without fulfilling Papa's dream of her becoming a Doctor, daunting as it was, soon gave way to deep sadness and anguish as she confronts the full extent of her mother's illness. Traumatized as she was, Barbara summons her inner strength to accept and live with her mother's creeping death. It tested her faith deeply. How can God, to whose Church and Ministry, she had dedicated her life, fail to answer her prayer and relieve her mother of the burden of disease? She tells us how the grief of her mother's illness and eventual passing, gave her the courage to endure pain without fear, to hope. It is the same courage she has brought to handling success and failure, love and rejection, marriage and motherhood, faith and renewal, friendships and enterprise.

From her zeal to preaching the good word as a child, to coping with the challenges of sisterhoods in a far-off land, to coping with contradictions of life as she came of age, falling in and out of love, as well as with grief over the loss of a loving mother, her rising and finding her feet, building lasting friendships and succeeding as a mother, a church elder, and now an entrepreneur, Barbara's life is anchored in prayer and her abiding faith in God. Faith is the cornerstone of SHAPED and its core message.

It is about how faith builds and transforms, how it empowers and conquers fear, how it inspires liberating truth that unburdens the heart, how it engenders strength to shoulders wearied down by tragedy, suffering and human failings, how it builds enduring friendships and fellowships, and how it builds resilience for success.

SHAPED is in many ways a tribute to the memory of her mother Laurette (La charmante), as it is a tribute to Papa Barnabe, who gave her sound grounding in early education, personal discipline, love of nation and patriotism, faith and allowed her the space to self-express and build confidence. Without such grounding, she would have struggled more to shoulder the burdens or to shine through the challenges and adversity described in SHAPED.

SHAPED is certainly not a definitive memoir. After all, at such a young age, Barbara still has a whole life before her. Indeed, as she says in the book, SHAPED, is a collection of some of her most compelling life experiences so far, which she wants to share in the hope that they will resonate and touch someone in similar circumstances or going through similar life challenges. She hopes that if the book contributes to the wellness of another human being, it will have achieved its purpose.

SHAPED is a book most of us can relate to. We have shared some, or maybe most of those Barbara's experiences. What is true is that most of us can situate ourselves in similar circumstances at some point in our lives. The lessons that Barbara's book brings to us and especially the young people is how to deal with the myriad of life challenges and adversity through faith, hard work, belief in oneself, and knowing when an opportunity knocks to build partnerships that endure and deliver success.

SHAPED is superbly written in simple flowing prose yet powerful in the delivery of its core message of faith. It is quite a good read. I hope the readers will find SHAPED as engaging and as useful as I did.

– Ambassador Musinga Timothy Bandora
(Uncle Tim), Dar es salaam, Tanzania

BANK OF KIGALI
Financially transforming lives

SHAPED BY LIFE

We are all shaped by life's circumstances and we believe in people's agency to determine their own destiny. At the Bank of Kigali, we are pleased to be part of the "OUR STORIES MATTER INITIATIVE" in partnership with ÉCLAT COMMUNICATIONS to launch their first book; "SHAPED". We want to empower Rwandans to tell their stories as storytelling is an obligation to future generations.

Rwandans' stories are as diverse as they are inspirational. A powerful quote goes: "We're all immortal, as long as our stories are told". Our hope is that through this initiative, Rwandans will share their stories of grief, resilience, hope, and stories of heroism, determination, revival, dignity, and love.

Today, a new generation of Rwandans, shaped by the remarkable leadership of His Excellency President Paul Kagame, is ready to play their rightful role to make Rwanda and indeed the world a better place. ÉCLAT COMMUNICATIONS will seek to support them to voice their opinions and tell their stories.

Dr. Diane Ngendo Karusisi
Chief Executive Officer
Bank of Kigali Plc, Rwanda

TIN No. 107610471 | KN4 Ave No 12, Kigali - Rwanda | (+250) 788 143 000 | bk@bk.rw | www.bk.rw

REVIEWS

In "Shaped" Barbara is honest and candid about both her highs and lows, her roses and her thorns - this makes her story very relatable and yet deeply challenging. A life shaped by strength, courage and grit from a young tender age! As you turn the pages of this book, you experience with Barbara the various incidents in her life: you pick a leaf from her successes, you learn from her mistakes and in the process we too are being "shaped" along with her. In the words of Henry David Thoreau, the American Poet, "Taking the path of least resistance, leads to crooked rivers and crooked men." Barbara's life story is littered with scenes where she chose the path of courage (especially while she lived in the United Kingdom), and not the path of least resistance...it did pay off through the shaping of her character into the bold, impactful woman she is today. Enjoy this read as I did.

– Shiphrah Kenganzi Kiiza
Team Leader at Redwoods Leadership

"SHAPED is an inspiring and refreshing book recommended for anyone who confronts challenging life problems and desires to learn and grow from them. This is a must read for the youths who want to pursue their dreams relentlessly."

– Prof. Silas Lwakabamba
Regional Managing Director at Coventry University Africa Hub

"Barbara's book is a full circle story about immigrating in search of new opportunities, grief, failure, outgrowing society's expectations of you as a woman, creating new opportunities in your own terms and resilience, lots of resilience. I hope many more women can tell their own stories, in their own voices."

– Nathalie Munyampenda
Educator, CEO of Kepler

"I stopped and closed this book a few times reading it. Too young to comprehend, but still too attentive to detail to know it would impact someone when she got older. I am very proud of you Barbara; this will be such a heartfelt addition to many households that would like a few years rewritten."

– Georgie Ndirangu,
Global Moderator

"Barbara's book is brilliantly written. She shares her life's journey with her readers, a journey filled with obstacles and hardships which have shaped who she is today. Despite the hardships she has overcome, she rarely expresses regret over her circumstances, rather she demonstrates how one can make the best out of life's most difficult moments. The woman she is today is a reflection of the education she has gained from her upbringing, family, past marriage, motherhood, and Christian walk. Reading this book, and receiving its rich and inspiring content is a privilege, a privilege I wish is received by every individual who picks up this book."

– Chantal Munanayire,
Institute for Economic Empowerment of Women
Rwanda Country Facilitator

"Barbara's book is an extension of her passion for people and serving God. The light given by her parents in her upbringing, guided and equipped her to deal with life's hardships and challenges while at the same time teaching her important life lessons that will assist others. I personally call her my little sister. As a woman of integrity, it cannot go without saying that, her intentional and consistent support to the survivors of the Genocide against the Tutsi is outstanding and commendable. This book, resonating from the force that was her mother, Laurette, is dedicated to all mothers who constantly strive for a better livelihood of their families. I hope you enjoy it as I did when reading it."

Charles Habonimana
Author of Moi, le dernier Tutsi,
Managing Director at Rwanda Airports Company

ACKNOWLEDGEMENTS

I would never have found the courage to sit, process and document my life in such a manner if it hadn't been for the strength, encouragement and constant motivation lent to me by some of my friends and family. For them, I am grateful that they never allowed me to give up or shelve this book.

I am so thankful to Rugasaguhunga Ruzindana who read the first chapter that I wrote, when we were all in the March 2020 COVID Lockdown, and straightaway lit my mind on fire, telling me that I had the potential to write.

This book would not be here if it wasn't for Obed Sean Musabe who literally drew a map for the publishing of this book. My friend and trusted business advisor, thank you for consistently showing me that every dream can become a reality, no matter how big and wild it is.

This book is all about my life experiences and the people, amongst many, who molded me to become who I am. I would not be who I am without my parents; Mpfizi Barnabé who, until this day shapes me and my dearly departed mother, Kantengwa Laurette who, despite leaving this world too soon, laid a strong foundation of the house that I am and hope to become. Thank you!

For ensuring that I lived a better life in England, Bishop Mukwiza Laurent, Pastors Felin and Dadali Josée Gakwaya, I am eternally grateful for you, thank you for adopting and loving me when I needed it most.

I would have never walked into my calling, stood upright and pursued God's vision for my life, if I had never met and served under the leadership of Apostle. Dr. Paul Gitwaza. Thank you for allowing God to use you in my life and pushing me to become the best version of myself from day one. "Thank you" will never be enough. The entrepreneur that I have become, the freedom that I enjoy while I pursue my dreams and the fulfilment that I get with each little breakthrough in this journey are all testaments of woman empowerment in my country, and for that, I am thankful for the visionary leadership that Rwanda has been blessed with.

Introduction to the Shaped Journey

A diary given; a passion born

It was the year 2000 when my mother approached me with a diary from the Bank of Kigali. That is where she worked for so many years. Mama had the habit of bringing home new year Bank of Kigali diaries every January, and gifting them to my father, her relatives and friends.

On one particular evening, she handed me a small diary and told me, "I think you should have one of these. Every evening before you sleep, write in it what has happened to you. Treat this as your special diary." It's on that evening that my passion to write was born.

Over the years, Mama continued to give me diaries, and I always tried my best to document my life and experience. Back then, there weren't any smartphones or a social media takeover. So, I stored my memories not in pictures and videos at the tip of my fingers, but in words written and safely tucked away in my Bank of Kigali diaries. My high school crushes were safely recorded, my teenage and emotion-based blunders were written down, and a piece of my soul was kept on those thin, long and beige pages.

I didn't know it then, but as I grew up and kept the habit, I realized that writing made me feel better. It became my safe space to express my feelings and process my thoughts. I documented my life experiences, my thoughts, my dreams, my fears, my loves and my aspirations.

Through this, I also discovered that I loved poetry. Poems became my tools for deep emotional expression when I became a hopeless romantic, and I wrote them whenever I fell in love.

Writing about my High School crushes transitioned to writing poems for the gentlemen that I admired, still keeping them to myself. Whenever I reflected on my relationships, my poems taught me so much about myself and my view of relationships at different stages of my life.

Fast forward to my early thirties, I was going through a divorce, I had to resort to trying therapy and it was there that I discovered that writing is a technique that counselors use to help their clients in processing their various issues and concerns.

Shortly after, the COVID-19 pandemic struck the world and like everyone else, I was stuck in my house under the lockdown measures imposed by the government to control the pandemic. I almost lost my mind. I couldn't leave the house and I couldn't go for therapy anymore. I was heartbroken and needed an outlet for my pain and anger.

So, I decided to get back to my passion for writing, except that this time, I wasn't writing in a Bank of Kigali diary I was using my laptop and to my amazement, in one hour, I had written five pages. I couldn't believe what had just happened. I was relieved but also surprised that I could write so much about myself in such a short space of time.

I read my pages and decided to share them with a friend and asked him for his thoughts on what I had just written. After a few minutes, he called me back and told me that I had the potential to write a book, and that there could have never been a greater time for me to sit still and actually start writing.

He challenged me to think big, and to think of publishing a book. Little did he know that he was reigniting a fire in me that was first lit when Mama gave me my first diary all those years back,

Over the course of the following weeks, still in lockdown, I made writing my full-time job and by the time the first portion of lockdown was lifted, I had written over 70% of this memoir. After the lockdown, I realized how much more of my personal experiences should actually be documented into a book. I looked back at how each of my life experiences shaped me to become the person I am today. All of a sudden, it dawned on me that perhaps, someone, somewhere could benefit from my life and experience. I knew then, that, such a contribution would be noble.

On that note, I am thrilled to present to you, SHAPED, a collection of some of my most vivid life experiences, both good and bad. As you read through the pages that depict parts of my life, allow me to speak to you through these words: Every act that you do on a daily basis, whether small or grand, holds so much weight both in the short term and in the long term. It will not only impact your life, but also shape those of the generations to come.

Barbara, the old soul

Of all the names that my parents could have given me, I have always wondered why Barbara is what they chose. It is not such a common name, and to be quite honest, it has always sounded like an old woman's name. Not cute at all, but that's what I was called.

When I was grown enough to ask the right questions, I asked my father why he and Mama named me Barbara, and his response was unexpected.

"Barbara, you were two weeks late. Your mother and I were taking a walk one evening when she complained, 'This girl should be named after an old woman because she is overdue. She will be an old soul.'

It's then that they decided that Barbara, taken after an elderly novelist, Barbara Cartland, was the right name for me.

On August 22nd 1986, at Roi Khaled Hospital, I finally showed up, healthy and strong, and made Mpfizi Barnabe Israel and Kantengwa Laurette first time parents together.

Shortly before that, my paternal grandfather had asked my father to name me 'Vastrose', before passing away in Tanzania where he lived. I was named "Vastrose" after a German colonialist friend of his who had worked with him in Rwanda. My parents however never recorded that name in official documents.

As this book was being edited and I shared some chapters with Papa, he realized that I had actually never known my original Rwandan name and decided to humor me. Apparently, when I born, I was originally named 'Musaniwabo' (Resembling her family) by my maternal grandmother. Basically, I was 35 years old when I discovered this! Ha! I couldn't believe it and neither should you, dear reader, feel the urge to jokingly call me 'Musaniwabo' next time we meet. I am expecting some jokes to come from this, so, do expect me to remind you that I explicitly wrote about you not calling me my newly discovered name.

So how did I get my 'Umuhoza' name, you ask. In January 1987, my parents decided to name me, 'Umuhoza' (Comforter) because I was born after the death of my grandfather.

There is a Rwandan proverb that says, "So ntakwanga. Akwita nabi" (Your father doesn't hate you. He just gives you a bad name), which means that the name your father gives you determines your destiny and where you end up in life. This proverb couldn't be truer for me.

Not only was it given to me to signify the comforting blessing of a daughter born after the recent death of her grandfather, but I have also noticed that I find myself attracted to people dealing with various life issues, with an unshakable need to help them.

I find great satisfaction in loving and helping people deal with challenges they face on a day-to-day basis. Perhaps it is because of my name. Perhaps it's what God created me for.

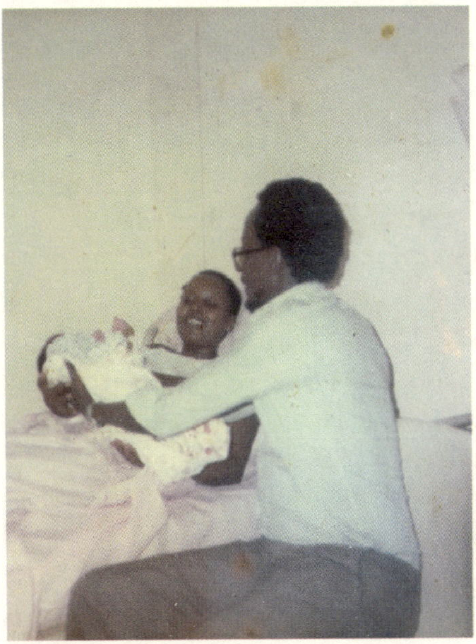

A few days after my birth, Papa hands me to Mama, who was still recovering from my birth.

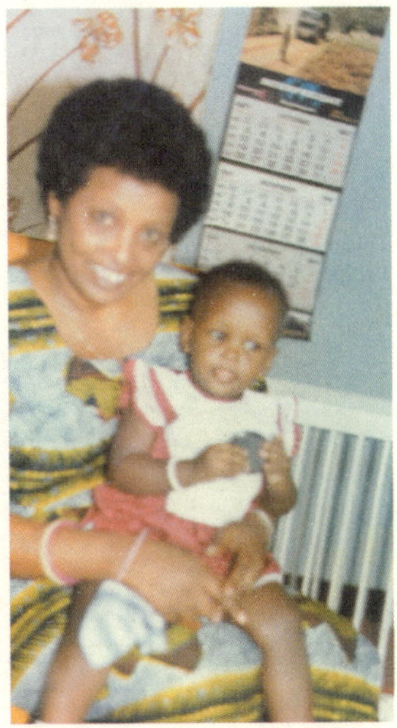

Mama carrying me in our small living room in Ngagara.

Standing next to Papa at an uncle's farm.

Historical Context

As known in the history of my country, Rwanda, many Tutsis lived in exile in neighboring countries prior to the 1994 Genocide against the Tutsi, and I was one of those children born in exile.

Mukaru yo mu Ngagara / The black tea of Ngagara

I was born in Bujumbura, Burundi, in Ngagara, 'Quartier Deux' (District Two), and like all children born in exile, growing up was bittersweet; bitter in the sense that due to our predicament, we didn't have all our needs comfortably met, and sweet in the sense that our families lived closely knit together, seen as outcasts, surviving with an unquenchable fire to return home, our dream land of a thousand hills.

We lived in poverty, but I didn't notice it then. I mean, I was a child and didn't know any better. We lived in a two-bedroom house with a tiny living room, and a maid's quarters outside. We survived a lot on "Mukaru yo mu Ngagara" (the black tea of Ngagara) and French baguette bread, just like it was said by people who made fun of the poverty that Rwandan exiles in Burundi lived in. From Papa's memory, 20 francs could buy you sugar, 10 francs bread and 5 francs a teaspoon of black tea powder and you would have your breakfast. To me, that was the best meal I could ask for. Our parents tried their best to give us their best. and there was more to life than worrying about Mukaru yo mu Ngagara.

We all shared the little possessions we had, amongst ourselves. If we cooked and neighbors did not have food, they came over for a meal, and vice versa. Our parents never let us, the children, feel unsafe or without enough to eat. The love we were shown and given made us feel like that was all we needed. Indeed, it was. With love, in addition to our "mukaru", we were fine.

We were not so poor that we could go to bed without food but again...that mukaru is well known amongst Rwandans who were exiled in Burundi and mostly lived in poverty.

For school, I attended a local nursery at a place called Sesinga. Of course, I can't recall that place today, but my early memories of that school were that it was a fun place to be. I met other Rwandan children there and there wasn't much to do besides playing a lot.

From the moment I could make sense of life as a child, besides knowing my name, I knew that I was of Rwandan origin. We upheld our culture with all its values. Not only did we speak Ikinyarwanda at home, coupled with its close cousin, Ikirundi, we also often heard our parents talk about our country, which was highly idealized in our household. Every evening, they would come home, talk about how their day went, check on us, have dinner and then sit to talk about Rwanda and the prospects of our return.

Rwanda was the promised land, the land of a thousand hills, and Rwanda was where our parents were born. Rwanda was Iwacu (our home) where we belonged. But we didn't live there, and as a child, I never really understood what had happened for us to end up in another land. In my mind, there was only so little that I could understand about the politics surrounding our livelihood, but my parents always found simple ways of explaining to us who we were and what had brought us to Burundi.

There wasn't much that they could share with us about our complex history, but soon enough, history would take a different turn.

1st October 1990

I was four years old when this day arrived and I remember something very distinctive about it; my parents were overjoyed! They came home from work with uncontrollable excitement.

"Do we have a party at home?" I wondered. "Is there a birthday to celebrate?"

With the limited resources that we had, we never missed birthday parties. They didn't require much then. A crate of Fanta, "ibitumbura" or donuts and a small cake were all we needed for a great party. But this day was different. There were none of those goodies, but the jubilant mood was the same. So, as inquisitive as I always was, I asked Mama what was making them so happy.

She answered simply, "Barbara, tugiye gutaha (Barbara, we are returning home)"

In my Kirundi, I responded; "Tuzotaha hehe (Where are we going)?" I inquired further. And her excited response was, "Tugiye kujya mu Rwanda (We're going to Rwanda)."

Yes, I knew that we were Rwandans and that there was this beautiful place called Rwanda, but I didn't know that moving there would bring so much excitement in our livelihoods. As time came, I began to understand why.

Inkotanyi

Just like I heard so much about Rwanda during those daily evening conversations in our household, I heard so much about Inkotanyi. The word was so famously used at home that it ignited my curious little mind so much, I had to find out who or what it was. And the day I asked my parents what it meant is the day that I caught the patriotic bug.

Mama, who would get excited every time she heard the word, 'Inkotanyi', took on the task of explaining as much and as best as she could about who the Inkotanyi were. "Barbara," she said, "Inkotanyi are our heroes. They are young men and women who are fighting for us to go back to Rwanda and live happily." Her answer elicited a conversation I'm sure she wasn't ready for.

Over the four years of that liberation struggle, I would often inquire, "Why are they fighting? Why are they fighting for us? Can't we just go back without fighting?" She would almost give a political explanation to a child's mind that really needed to make sense of all the information she was getting. "Inkotanyi are fighting for us to return because we are Tutsis who have lived in exile for so many years, and the Hutus who live in Rwanda do not want us to go back and live with them. We can't go back without fighting because we have tried and they have refused. Barbara, always pray that they win because when they win, we will go back home," she explained. To this explanation, I would get even more confused and ask, "Mama, who are Tutsis? Who are Hutus? What is the difference?"

At this point, Papa would step in the conversation and explain some more, "Barbara, Rwandans are somehow different. The Hutu sent the Tutsi out of Rwanda. The Tutsi who left have been living bad lives. There are also other Tutsis who stayed in Rwanda, but they too are not safe."

Knowing that I would eventually probe for more, he would usually conclude the discussion and say, "Barbara, you are still too young to understand some of these things. You will know more as you grow up. For now, just pray for Inkotanyi. If they win, we all win."

Having been raised with the simple understanding that God loved children so much and that He always answered their prayers, I took on the assignment to pray for Inkotanyi. These superheroes, as Mama portrayed them, needed my prayers and I was going to pray for them until they won, because if they won, we would finally go back home and my parents would always be as happy as they were on birthday parties.

Mama (2nd from the right) with her friends and some Inkotanyi soldiers. She visited the frontlines quite a number of times.

Radio Muhabura

Every evening, besides the conversations about Rwanda and Inkotanyi, precious time was devoted to listening to Radio Muhabura. Besides the Burundi National radio, it was the only one we listened to at home. We would all gather around our small black and metallic radio, and listen to the updates of the war, along with the motivational music that played after each news and program segment.

This was a special time for us, it created a sense of togetherness and hope for us, all our family members and other Rwandans living in exile. Some evenings, aunties and uncles would come to our house and listen to the radio together with my parents, and after the news, they would then proceed to arguing and debating on which way the war could go, what needed to be done and what each Rwandan could do. They loved the stories of victory.

I can still hear Mama's joyous laugh every time she would hear great news from the frontline, and her exclamations, "Nuko sha! Mubatsinde (Yes, keep it up. Defeat them)!" Her electric joy would be the highlight of our evenings alongside Radio Muhabura broadcasts.

Radio Muhabura had a way of creating morale in the hearts of Rwandans, hope for the future and a sense of belonging to something bigger than exile. Indeed, the liberation struggle was the only viable option for Rwandans in exile to fulfill the dreams that they dreamt for a while.

I remember seeing how my parents' faces would light up when they would hear of the victories of Inkotanyi. On most nights, where there was a conquered area, Mama would play some Cecile Kayirebwa or Muyango songs on our small cassette player and dance. The victories were for all of us. I was too young to understand what these victories meant but I just knew that some good news would have passed on Radio Muhabura to get Mama dancing.

We didn't listen to Radio Muhabura during the evenings only. As a matter of fact, the radio would be on even during the day. On days that I would be at home, I would listen to it with my little brother and our Rwandan maids, to whom the liberation struggle was also a personal matter.

Listening to the radio so often opened my mind to great imagination and I picked an interest in news and storytelling at that young age. I then developed a habit of recounting the news I would have heard, and in the evenings, when Mama and Papa came home, I would be there to update them and tell them what they had missed during the day.

I was quite an entertaining six-year-old 'journalist'. I mixed stories, some of which I got right, and others, I just used my wild imagination. But in the end, my audience loved my stories. To this day, some of my aunties have never forgotten the six-year-old chatterbox that I was.

Rwanda, here we come!

Our journey back to Rwanda didn't start with the end of the 1994 Genocide against the Tutsi. Our journey back to our motherland began on the fateful day when the Burundian President, Melchior Ndadaye was assassinated in October 1993.

As a child, I didn't know much about the circumstances surrounding his death, but I can remember the fear and dread that my parents had. As much as they tried so hard to hide it from us, I distinctly remember the uncomfortable feeling of uncertainty in our little house. Each day, my parents would tell each other, "Iyaba urugamba rwarangiraga vuba tugataha iwacu i Rwanda" (If only the liberation struggle would end soon so that we return to Rwanda)!"

Fear-struck conversations between my parents only served to get more worried. The conversations that my parents had with our relatives and friends gave me a sense of dread, that with my little comprehension, I believed that since we were Tutsis, we would never be accepted anywhere, we would always be hunted and we would eventually die. I was afraid to lose my parents and my brother, and to die. My parents talked about the liberation struggle as our only way out and this just got me anxious. I remember that as a child, I kept telling God, "Help the Inkotanyi. Please help us not to die. I am scared of dying." They had to make it or else, we would always live in fear. Spine chilling fear.

Things got worse in Bujumbura. My parents couldn't go back to work, bullets flew over our neighborhood and our house, and death was knocking on so many doors. When the bullets started hitting houses, Papa decided we wouldn't be sleeping on our beds anymore, but on the floor instead. That way, stray bullets would miss us. In the night, we would all huddle together on one mattress and hope to wake up alive the next morning.

During the night, bullets were flying over the house, non-stop. People were screaming from afar and at the same time, Papa and Mama were holding us tight so that we could sleep but I could feel Papa's heart pump fast. As a child, I found comfort in the embrace of our parents but I couldn't help but wonder, what had we done to be living in this fear? I was too young to comprehend the whole situation but I never lost the sense of anxiety since then.

The flats of Muyenga Tank Hill

Rwandans lived in constant fear for their lives in those times and the liberation struggle wasn't going as fast as they would have wished. Amidst the political turmoil however, my father managed to apply for a job at the UNICEF office in Kampala, Uganda, and got the job.

After some weeks, the situation in Burundi stabilized and life started looking like it would get back to normal. In a few months, my father then moved to Kampala and got settled. Shortly after, my mother went there to visit and to check on how soon we could all move there. While they were gone, we stayed with some aunties, and after a week, Mama came back and told us to pack our bags because we were all moving to Kampala, Uganda.

We could not contain our excitement, especially that we were going to be flying on a plane to Kampala! The journey of going to the airport and boarding a flight became the highlight of the whole trip. Eventually, the day came. Mama packed all our clothes in the new suitcases that she had brought from Kampala. She called all our closest family members who were living in Bujumbura to come and see us off. We shared lunch, said our goodbyes to our cousins and were ready to go to the airport. I remember my maternal grandparents telling us, "Tuzabonanira mu Rwanda (We shall meet again in Rwanda)." It's then that I understood that Uganda was simply a stop-over, and the final destination would eventually be Rwanda.

At the airport, my little brother and I were excited. Mama checked us in with our passports, took us to the waiting area, and waited until we were notified via the loudspeakers that it was our time to board. We stood up and made our way to the doors and went outside, walked the tarmac and waved back at the family members who stood over us on the airport towering balcony.

We were awestruck by the sheer size of the plane. We climbed the stairs, entered inside and were shown our seats by the flight attendants. The flight was a short one. We soon landed on an even bigger airport; Entebbe International Airport. Mama took our hands and led us through the customs, and we then proceeded to pick our luggage. We proceeded to the waiting area, where Papa was waiting for us with open arms and a beaming smile on his face. We both jumped into his arms and could finally feel safe.

Papa hugged and kissed Mama, and told us that he was so happy that we were finally back together again. He told us that he had come with his car to pick us up at the airport. His car? Papa had a car!

It was a white Toyota Corolla and he had a driver named David. As we made our way to the car, I could already feel our life getting much better than what we had been used to in Ngagara. To my amazement, we had a car of our own. A small refugee family from Ngagara suddenly owned a car in Kampala! Life was indeed changing for the better.

We sat in the car and made our way to our new home. Of course, on the way, I had a few questions to ask; "What's the name of the place where we are going to live, Papa?"

"It is called Muyenga Tank Hill," he replied. "Now put your curiosity on hold. We'll arrive there soon."

We pulled on a strip of four new flats, and one of them was where we would live. We pulled up in the garage and immediately my brother and I jumped out of the back seat and went to the front of the house, and we could barely take it all in!

"Barbara, you will check out the house tomorrow morning. Let's go inside now," called out Papa. We obeyed excitedly and went into the house.

The house was nothing like I had ever seen before in my life. The living room was spacious, with brand new sofas, a dining table and a balcony. There was a corridor from the garage through to the kitchen, which was tiled and brand new. It was equipped with a new electric cooker, a new fridge full of food, and new tableware. Everything was new. It was definitely another life. My parents were happy looking at our bewildered faces. We were like kids in a candy store that had just been bought by their parents.

Papa told us that he wanted to show us upstairs and we couldn't wait. We ran up the stairs and he showed us our bedroom first. The size must have been larger than our living room in our little previous house. There was a neatly laid bed with new sheets, a spacious cupboard where we could keep our clothes, a large window overlooking the tarmac road that passed in front of our gate, and a neatly cut garden beneath our bedroom.

He then took us to the bathroom we would be using. This was a foreign concept for me since, in Ngagara, we would take our showers outside the house in the open or, if it ever rained, in the kitchen where everyone would be passing me and my brother and tickling or teasing us.

Papa then took us to his and Mama's bedroom, and told us that if we needed anything, we could knock on their door and ask. The master bedroom was self-contained and even more spacious than our own room. It had a large bed, also neatly made, and a dressing mirror for Mama that stood opposite the bed, just across a large window.

Finally, he showed us the guest room where our guests would be spending the night whenever they would be coming over to visit us.

Once the house tour was completed, Mama gave us a shower, got us in our nightwear, and then we had a warm, delicious meal which we washed down with soft drinks.

Life in this Muyenga Tank Hill flat was going to be heaven on Earth.

Buganda Road Primary School

Since we were going to stay in Kampala for a while, Papa had to get us settled in a good school. We went to look for a school and among the schools that we visited were Nakasero Primary School and Buganda Road Primary school.

In the end, the best option, according to Papa, was Buganda Road Primary school. He registered me right away, but decided to take my little brother to another kindergarten that was closer to our house.

At Buganda Road Primary school, I was given school materials, uniform and a list of other necessities that I would need for the term. Once the registration was completed, we set off to buy everything I needed at Owino market, and we prepared for school.

I joined Primary Two and studied there up to Primary Three, when we had to leave Kampala to return to Rwanda. Coming from a Francophone system and changing to an Anglophone system was challenging. Papa had to get a tutor for us at home to teach us English and help us understand what was being taught at school. It is true, children learn fast and soon enough, but our tutor made it more engaging and, in a few months, we caught up.

My closest friends were two Rwandan girls, Umutoni Brenda and Bwiza Gloria. We don't know how it happened, but we connected on the first day we met. When we discovered that we were Rwandan, we felt like we were meant to stand up for each other. We always had each other's backs and we always helped each other with school work.

Umutoni Brenda was the smartest of us all. She aced each subject and we never knew how she pulled it off. As Rwandans, we felt so proud that she shined. There was something about being Rwandan and raised Rwandan in exile that made us proud of each other's accomplishments. I remember Papa asking me one day who was the top of our class and when I mentioned that she was a Rwandan girl, he smiled.

We can't eat fish anymore

Everyone who lives in Kampala knows that people there love to eat fish. Fish was affordable and during the weekend, we would buy some by Lake Victoria and take home. Our cook would have different ways to cook it but my favorite was the fried fish. Fried fish and chips with some Ketchup sauce on the side was a delicacy. When guests came to visit, fish was always on the table. My mother loved to eat the fish with "Ubugali" and a red sauce, but for us, fish was tastier when accompanied by chips. Then, one terrible day came, and we couldn't eat fish anymore.

One morning, while watching TV with Papa in the living room, news passed that the airplane that was carrying President Juvenal Habyarimana of Rwanda had been shot down and mass killings of the Tutsi in Rwanda ensued. The plan to detail Genocide against the Tutsi in Rwanda began, and every living Tutsi outside the country knew that the apocalypse had begun. Tutsis were being massacred in Rwanda, bodies were being thrown in the Nyabarongo river and making their way to Lake Victoria and the fish in the lake had feasted on the bodies of our loved ones. So, for a long time, we couldn't eat fish.

I remember asking Papa one day; "Papa, why haven't we gone to the lake to buy fish? I miss eating fish." And I vividly remember him telling me; "Barbara, we can't eat fish anymore because the fish have eaten our people."

It really didn't sink in my little child's mind but the pain in Papa's eyes while telling me those words and the fact that we couldn't eat fish for a long time made me realize that something terrible had happened.

When the Genocide began, Mama had gone back to Bujumbura to check on our families there, and we stayed with Papa. Every waking moment that he was at home, he watched the news, glued to the screen as the gruesome images of people being butchered were shown.

"Papa, why are they hurting people every day?" I asked, to which he responded, "They are killing people for no reason at all. They are killing them because they are Tutsi like us." Those words frightened me so much and took me back to our little home in Ngagara when President Ndadaye was assassinated. Papa was very sad. He was detached and I could see that this was actually worse than what happened when we were in Burundi.

As a child, I remember feeling that we would never be safe, whether in a tiny house in Ngagara with bullets flying over our small house or in our flat in Muyenga. There was something I could not make sense of a child but to me; being Tutsi carried fear and it was paralyzing.

In hindsight, I shouldn't have seen those images on TV but again Papa was in so much pain to notice that I and my young brother Aggrey were watching TV with him. On TV, I saw children of my age crying for their mothers., Mothers crying for their children, men hacked, too shocked to speak, and blood flowing like rivers on the streets frightened me and broke my little heart. This could have been us.

When Papa was watching the news, I wanted to both watch the news and not watch the news. I was so curious but I was so afraid. In my mind, there was one main question; "What was wrong with being Tutsi?"

Even in Kampala, my parents never stopped to cheer for Inkotanyi and thus, I asked Papa about Inkotanyi, "Could they stop the horrors that I saw on TV?" to which he answered; "Barbara, Inkotanyi need more of your prayers now because things are very bad."

This wasn't enough as an answer but he must have believed that our prayers could help them. But Barbara couldn't stop thinking; "What if they couldn't stop it and the killers would finish all the Tutsi in Rwanda and then come over to Uganda and finish us all? Were we being kept for the slaughter too? If Tutsis were not safe then, I would never be safe. If we didn't have the Rwanda that we so longed for, then we would never belong anywhere else in the world.

Indeed, things were bad. In a matter of weeks, mutilated bodies were thrown in rivers and lakes, and soon made their way to Lake Victoria in Uganda. The TV news informed the general public that people couldn't eat fish anymore because the fish had fed on these corpses.

Sheltering family and friends

The following weeks after the beginning of the Genocide against the Tutsi, some Rwandans managed to flee to neighboring countries. Some of those who made it to Kampala moved in with us. With the situation in Burundi being quite volatile too, cousins, aunties and uncles from there moved in with us as well. It was such a great time to have our house full. It just felt more warm and lively.

It was quite a shift in our lives but according to the Kinyarwanda proverb, "Aho umwaga utari uruhu rw'urukwavu rwisasira batanu," which loosely translates to, where there is no selfishness, the rabbit skin will comfortably cover more than five people. Our home became a rabbit skin for some months.

Our house was a space of two great feelings; solace and fear. Solace because our relatives were sheltered from the dangers of what was happening in Burundi and Rwanda and fear because of exactly that same reason. In the mornings, we would all have breakfast together, the table would be full of laughter, jokes and much more. My brother and I being the kids in the house; we were dotted on a lot. I loved the affection in the morning before going to school. Some days, not all the cousins would be up but an adult was always up to have breakfast with us. We would come back from school in the evening and find everyone at home. When we came home, everyone would be happy to see us. Some days, we would watch our favorite Looney Tunes with the cousins who found our attention to the animations fascinating. On other days, they would watch the news with us sitting by the dining table. I didn't like the solemn faces that all the adults would have once the news would come on. At some point, when the news came on, one of the aunties or cousins would hurriedly take us out of the living room to one of the bedrooms so as to shield us from the gruesome images on TV but instantly, as kids, we would feel a change in the ambiance at home.

My brother was still very young that he really didn't know what was happening, besides, all that Aggrey wanted to do was play, play and play.

Day in, day out, our house was bustling with activity and life. If conversations were not filled with Genocide stories and Inkotanyi victories, they were full of jokes. These were among the best times of my life.

Losing Uncle Rutayisire Narcisse

Rutayisire Narcisse was my father's eldest brother. He lived in present day Eastern Province, Rwanda, in Rwamagana. He had visited us in Burundi and had tried to get us to visit his family in Rwanda on so many occasions but given the unpredictability of the politics in Rwanda, Papa was wary of visiting. Still, Uncle Rutayisire insisted that we visit. He would write letters to Papa and tell him that there was nothing much to worry about, he trusted that his integrity and good relations in the community were enough for the protection of his family. In those days, only hand written letters were the main mode of communication. Uncle Rutayisire wrote so many letters to Papa, asking about us all, my grandparents and how life in exile was treating us. He was a very loving man.

Prior to the Genocide however, after the insistence of Uncle Rutayisire, Papa seriously reconsidered visiting Rwanda. He then planned and visited Uncle Rutayisire and his family. On another occasion, our grandmother also visited and stayed with Uncle and his family for almost a year. His family was everything to him. He lived only for his family and for us. He never stopped talking about us, our family and the whole family in Tanzania. That's what was dearest to his heart.

For some time, Uncle Rutayisire insisted that Papa take all of us to visit him and Papa had reached a point whereby he wanted us to visit so that he could make his brother happy but also get our families to meet. Getting to know our cousins was something that he really wanted, since we had never lived with that part of our family. When the Genocide began, on April 16th he was killed, as were all his Tutsi friends from Rwamagana.

In Kampala, I remember Papa glued to the TV, so worried, so afraid for his brother. There was absolutely no way of knowing who had lived or who had survived but some evenings, while watching the news, Papa kept telling my uncles who lived with us then; "What if Rutayisire doesn't survive this horror? What will happen to his family?" Some days, Papa would just sit in the sitting room, quiet and sad. I could feel his sadness but of course, he couldn't tell me why he was sad. It was beyond my understanding. From Papa's accounts of him, he was the perfect gentleman, full of humor and so much love for his extended family that lived in exile. When I grew up, I was told that he loved me so much and couldn't wait for all of us to visit him back home. From the testimonies of his children, he was a wise and intelligent gentleman. When they were young, Uncle Rutayisire, as advanced as he was at the time, had opened savings accounts for all his children; planning ahead for their education. He was an intentional parent and a loving husband to Aunt Melanie; who to this day still talks about how affectionate he was and still shares the memorable moments spent with him.

Uncle Rutayisire Narcisse (RIP), killed in the 1994 Genocide against the Tutsi.

One day, after the Genocide, news reached Papa that Uncle Rutayisire had been killed in Rwamagana but his family had survived. That was a terrible week! Papa couldn't leave our parents' room for some days and members of our family didn't know what to do to help. Mama was in Burundi with our families, getting ready to move back to Rwanda and we didn't know what to do. I felt sad. Sad that Papa was sad but also sad that we would never meet the loving elder brother of Papa that he fondly liked to talk about.

The loss of Uncle Rutayisire is one that we have always lived with and never got over. He was the lovely uncle, brother and friend that we never met; alongside the million and more lives that were snatched from us. I devoted his memory in my life because I do not want to forget about him nor do I want my children and you readers to not ever know that he lived. May his memory be a blessing.

Inkotanyi, the victors

The atrocities taking place in Rwanda were broadcasted all over the world just as updates on the liberation were also spreading like wildfire in the Rwandan communities. In every home, there was a radio blasting out loud Radio Muhabura, motivating its audience and exciting them to look forward to the ultimate victory. It was a complex situation.

On one hand, Tutsis were excited to return home. On the other hand, their families were hacked like lambs in a slaughterhouse. I was confused, being exposed to all that was going on. I wondered if we would find anyone left if we ever returned to Rwanda. Who would show us around? Who would tell us what life had been like before what I saw on the news?

We kept hoping, and the news were complex too. We were winning, yet we were losing our people. At each waking moment, we had to know how far Inkotanyi had reached but we had to watch the news to also see the estimated numbers of deaths. My family would cheer briefly but be brought down to their knees by the bodies spewn on the roads and the children shocked by what their eyes had seen.

Then one day, it was all over. They won!

Mama called us from Burundi and the excitement in her voice matched that in Papa's. We were finally going back to Rwanda. To be quite honest, I was so confused. My parents were happy and at the same time uncertain of what they would find back home. Papa told us that we were going to go back home to the land of milk and honey, Rwanda, but it would be different from what I had grown to love in Muyenga Tank Hill.

My little mind thought; "What if something goes wrong and we get killed?" "What if it's all a lie and Rwanda isn't as beautiful as what my parents told me? What would happen if I saw dead bodies? Blood on the roads?"

I was anxious. Anxious to see Mama and our families from Bujumbura again, but also afraid that something could go wrong and we could get killed too.

The excitement in our Muyenga home was palpable but on one hand, I was sad. The uncles, aunties and cousins would all move out and go back to their families and we would be a small family again.

On the other hand, Papa couldn't wait for us to go visit Rwanda. He told us that we would visit at first and then permanently move back once all was settled. Mama on the other end was getting ready to move for good with all the family members that had stayed in Burundi. Aunties, uncles and cousins all over Kampala constantly said, "Imfura zacu zatsinze. Turatashye (Our noble ones have won. We are going home)."

As a child, I really didn't understand the magnitude of what this victory meant but at least, we wouldn't see any more dead bodies on TV. At least, I wouldn't see the sadness in Papa's eyes each day that he watched the news. As a child, I thought, "If this is true, then there would be no fear of death coming for us wherever we would be as Tutsis."

In the weeks after that victory, a mass exodus began.

On the road to a better life

In August 1994, Papa drove with David, our driver from Kampala to Kigali. He reconnected with Mama who had also come to check on the situation and the possibility of returning back with the whole family from Burundi.

In November 1994, we got our chance to finally visit Rwanda. David drove us from Kampala to Kigali for what seemed like a month. We slept on the way, woke up, slept, woke up again, until we stopped counting. Every time we woke up, we asked Papa, "Are we there yet?" and he'd tell us where we were; "We just got out of Kampala," "We are near Masaka," "We will be in Mbarara soon," "Oh, we are close to Kabale. When we get there, we will be near Gatuna, which is where Uganda ends and Rwanda begins. Once we get to the border, I will wake you up so that you can see Rwanda as we drive through."

On that long drive, he kept us motivated by making short stops along the road and buying us grilled meat and maize. This was quite an experience.

We were eating food that we had not cooked along the road and Papa didn't seem to mind. Apart from the seemingly month-long drive, it was fun.

We eventually reached the border in Gatuna, and Papa woke us up. It was starting to get dark. There were many cars, buses and mini trucks full of people with their belongings. From the window of our white Toyota Corolla, I could see some people moving by. Some people were moving fast, going to get their documents checked like Papa had done, others were sad, some were smiling, others were quiet, it was a combination of many feelings. On every face I saw, there was a smile. I didn't exactly know why then, but I could see that everyone was happy and full of relief.

Papa went to get our travel documents checked and returned a few minutes later telling us that everything was in order and we would be on our way. It was another long drive. It was dark and there were no street lights. It was eerily quiet. There was nothing for me to see, so I fell asleep again.

I woke up when we entered the parking space in front of a dark house that had a few candles lit inside. Oh no! There was no electricity in this land of milk and honey. How could this be? Had my parents lied to us? All these thoughts dissipated the moment I saw Mama come out of the house to greet us; I was relieved. I had missed her so much and her warm embrace was comforting. My parents were relieved. It looked like they had carried so many heavy sacks of rice on their backs like the Owino market boys and now, they didn't have to carry them anymore.

This dark house was a house that Mama had gotten us in a move known as "kubohoza" or taking over something that doesn't belong to you. It was empty, so empty and haunted. It was in Kimihurura and it had four bedrooms. It was so dark and right then, right there, I wondered again, "why did my parents promise something that wasn't true?" I felt sad and scared. It was comforting that we were with our parents but it didn't change the fact that this Rwanda scared me. The darkness was too heavy and I right away missed the ambience and safety of our home in Muyenga Tank Hill.

My brother, Aggrey, was too young to connect what was happening, besides, he being a Mama's boy, seeing Mama was all that he needed right then. My parents were simply relieved that we were together again as a family and in Rwanda.

Once inside, the darkness in that empty looted house immediately contradicted the hope that I saw on my parents' faces. To them, this was going to be a very long journey that would end up in a better life. To me, it wasn't the heaven I had been promised.

Empty Streets, Empty Homes

We spent our first night in the same room as our parents but on different mattresses. Old and rugged mattresses that mom had laid on clean sheets for us. There were no beds, no pillows, just those mattresses and bedsheets. As I laid on the bed that night, I couldn't help but wonder, what was this? Why had we even come to this place that has no beds?!

The next morning, I was in for another shock. I woke up to an eerie quiet with a heavy sense of loss looming over. There was an emptiness that I couldn't explain. Very Scary. Very Sad.

Mama called my name; "Barbara, wake up, it's time for a shower and then you come for breakfast." I sluggishly woke up and hugged her that morning as I passed by her to go to the living room to pick my bag.

As I walked, a terrible smell kept rising the closer I came to the room. I remember gagging. It wasn't a smell I was familiar with at all. Reaching in the living room, the walls were stained with big splashes of a dark maroon color. What was this? What had happened in this house? I felt tears sting my eyes as I was completely bewildered and I let out a loud scream.

Mom rushed and carried me out of the living room and took me back to the room where we had spent the night. As I sat on the mattress, I didn't know which questions to ask. And she quietly stared at me. The curious little Barbara was buried under the overwhelming confusion and dread. "I don't want to be here," I remember my own heart saying to me as loud as it could.

But I just stared at my mother, as she stared back at me.

Mama and Papa seemed to not have the right answers to the questions that I couldn't stop asking. As much as they seemed helpless in getting us to understand, they confused me even more. As a child, I found our living conditions unpleasant compared to what I was accustomed to in Kampala and I didn't know why we had even come to this place. On the other hand, I still couldn't ignore the fact that my parents' joy was refreshingly constant. They seemed not to notice what my eyes saw; or rather; it didn't have much importance to them.

Finding food was a challenge, but good enough, we had brought with us some bread, milk, sugar, potatoes, bananas, beans, rice, onions and tomatoes from Kabale. We had also packed some household utensils such as saucepans, plates, cups and spoons. Mama would cook for us but it was obvious that life wouldn't be comfortable.

In the evenings, we would drive around the abandoned city, moving and bouncing on the dirt roads, looking for any place that was lively with people. One evening, we stumbled upon open bars in Remera. We stepped out of the car and lo and behold, we met some family friends celebrating their return to the country. Drinks and barbecue meat were being served, jokes went around, victory chant songs blasted on a cassette player in the corner, and adults celebrated as if they had won the lottery.

Being together with a group of people in those few hours lightened the ghost-like feeling that enveloped the whole country. Houses were soulless, roads were deserted, and in some parts, there was nothing but debris from the fighting. When it was time to leave the bar, we would all go back home to our empty homes; to the darkness and silence.

Jammed together

After two weeks stay in Kigali, we drove back to Kampala. Papa had resolved to start planning to leave his work and move the whole family to Kigali for good, and Mama returned to Burundi to find ways to bring a few remaining household items as well as assist our extended family in returning to Rwanda.

Our family in Bujumbura packed all their belongings and made their way back to the land that they had last seen some decades ago and us in Kampala, we returned to finish the academic year and started to plan our return home. Life was normal, predictable even, but the regular activities we were accustomed to were not as many. The house that was full of family members was now empty. Upon our return, the members of our family who had been living with us departed for Rwanda right away. In different parts of Kampala, many family friends began the exodus back to Rwanda. As a child, though I hadn't enjoyed the uncomfortable living conditions of Kigali, I missed Mama's laugh and the presence of tranquility that my parents shared back then. So, as everyone was leaving, it felt as though we were being left behind, in comfort but alone.

In 1995, we finally moved back to Kigali for good, leaving Papa behind. He stayed alone in Kampala for the last leg of his job contract at UNICEF. In Kigali, we stayed in another house that my mother had found.

We stayed with five whole families from Mama's side in a four-bedroom house. We were not less than thirty people, we were literally jammed like sardines in a can imported from Europe.

Our grandparents had their own bedroom. The aunties and uncles had their own bedrooms as well, and the children slept on mattresses in one room and in the living room. Food was served on extra-large platters, and since no amount of forks or spoons could have been sufficient for us, we all washed our hands and ate together. The younger children were fed separately, but everyone else had to eat what they could get their hands on.

Though I loved spending time playing with my cousins, and hearing stories from our grandfather, I didn't like the meal times. I wasn't a lazy eater, but I wasn't fast either. I easily got distracted like every nine-year old and would forget that food was for those who ate fast. As a result, I was never full and when I got left behind, I would always run to eat from Mama's plate.

This life was new to us, but despite our living conditions, Mama did a great job in keeping us emotionally safe. She tried her best to make the transition smooth, always encouraging us and telling us that we were fine as long as we were with her. As reassuring as mothers are, she gave us stability.

Foundations built

Yes, life in Rwanda was not easy, but we had an opportunity to live as Rwandans in our own country. With time, we had the privilege of slowly building our lives.

Soon enough, Papa's contract in UNICEF ended and instead of reapplying for a renewal, he decided to come back and stay with us in Rwanda for good. At this point, Mama had a job, working in the Credit and Loans department at the Bank de Kigali. We went back to school and attended Camp Kigali Primary School, where we were fortunate to find that it had both Anglophone and Francophone systems.

At this point, we had all moved from the house in Kimihurura, and almost all our families had eventually found houses to rent in Kigali. We settled in Niboye, Kicukiro with Mama's sister and her family for a few months, before she too moved out to her own house.

It is then that the nuclear family life came back to normal.

Chapter One

Shaped By Parents

My parents came from different backgrounds, but one thing was common for both of them; they both grew and lived in exile. Papa and his family were exiled in Tanzania whereas Mama's were exiled in Burundi in the 1950s. Their lives were not as easy as for all the Tutsi living in exile. Education and employment opportunities were close to none for them.

Papa's scenario in Tanzania was slightly different from that of Mama, who in her case, Rwandans had to open their own school - École St. Albert in Bujumbura to educate children from exiled families.

Being the firstborn daughter made me the focus of my parents' love, affection, and discipline. However, they played bad cop/good cop at different times when it came to raising me. I was such a daddy's girl, making him the good cop, and that meant that he spoiled me. Mama on the other hand, was often the bad cop who always called me out for being too spoiled and disciplined me. However, on average, she gave me more affection than discipline.

My fierce Rwandan refugee mother

From an early age, my mother was what I would call in layman terms, a hustler. She was a young woman living in a refugee camp but who studied, got a job and worked her way out of the refugee camp without leaving her family behind.

In her early twenties, Mama had managed to finish her high school education and got a job at the BCB (Banque du Crédit de Bujumbura). In her late twenties, she had taken out a mortgage from the bank and bought her first home in Bujumbura, and was using her whole salary to sustain her parents and pay for her siblings' tuition.

I mean, this woman, had she been born on the right side of history, she would have accomplished so much for herself, family and nation.

Money Matters – Being content

One of my distinctive childhood memories was when Mama taught me an important lesson the hard way. I was playing outside our house with my little brother, Aggrey, who Mama nicknamed, "Bahinja (Baby)." A stranger passed by and me being me, I engaged him in a conversation. I asked him where he was going and what he was going to do there. I must have been five years old but since I was quite the old soul from day one, talking was never a problem for me. This stranger found me interesting and asked me what I wanted him to buy me. Being a child, of course I asked for sweets. Since there wasn't a shop nearby, he decided to leave me a coin of 5 Burundian francs. This was the first piece of money that I ever held in my hands.

I immediately imagined buying loads and loads of sweets. I imagined spending the rest of my life never lacking sweets…Oh, how sweet it is to be a child. A few minutes later, Aggrey and I went back to the house, took a shower, dressed up in our pyjamas, had dinner and were taken to sit with Mama and Papa for a few minutes before going to bed.

I had my coin with me the whole time, making sure that I would always have sweets for the rest of my life. Mama noticed it and she paused and asked me, "Barbara, who gave you that coin?" I responded, "A man I do not know passed by and gave me the coin to buy sweets." Mama couldn't believe it. She quickly grabbed the coin from my hands and pulled me aside, gave me a good whooping before sitting me down.

I screamed my lungs out, pleading with Papa to somehow step in and ask her to stop beating me, but he didn't. Mama's piercing look towards him clearly said, "don't get involved," and he respected that.

As I sat, she came to me and told me, "Barbara, haven't I always told you to never take anything that is not yours?" To which I nodded my head in approval of that lesson. She continued to say; "It is wrong to ask for money from strangers. It is wrong to take money from people that you do not know. It is wrong to beg and you should be satisfied with what you have. I, your father, aunties and uncles are the only ones who can buy you sweets…No one else. Before taking money from anyone, tell them that we have forbidden you from taking money from them. OK?"

That lecture, as I would like to call it, is one of the greatest lessons I learned about contentment, self-respect and worth. It's from that incident that I learned to be content with the little that I have, and not be quick to look for ways to get things from people just for my temporary satisfaction.

To this day, I find it so hard to borrow money from people. I will only borrow if it's absolutely necessary and if it's the only way. And even then, I borrow from my closest friends and family members. It's always quite a process for me to reach a point of asking for money. That evening, Mama taught me that not every "gift" should be accepted, and that it was fine to actually turn them down. That was that, and it was settled then.

The Giver

On the flip side however, Mama was such a giver. Her being a social butterfly, she was always expected to draw people to our house for weekend visits. Weekends were always lively. If not for guests coming over for long hours, we'd visit family members and friends.

On multiple occasions also, she bought and packed a lot of food in different plastic bags to give to our vulnerable family members and friends. And every year, we gathered our used clothes that were still in good condition and donated them to the less fortunate. Mama never allowed us to wear clothes for too long to not be donated.

Mama taught us the value in relationships and what it meant to love other people beyond ourselves. Giving was her greatest strength.

The Patriot - A tribute to my mother

I was raised a patriot from the moment that I could learn how to talk, in the sense that, my first exposure to my roots was the use of our mother tongue, Ikinyarwanda in our home. I was taught to love my mother tongue and use it unashamedly. I was taught that our culture was rich and so deep that I didn't need to borrow other foreign customs. I was trained to dance as a means of expressing the grace of who we are as a strong and resilient people. I was raised by a strong Rwandan woman. I was raised Rwandan.

Benimpuhwe

Whenever I get the opportunity to meet and introduce myself to people who knew my parents, I tell them, "I am Laurette and Barnabe's daughter," and the response from them is always the same; "Oh wow! Your mother was very beautiful, and such a gifted dancer."

Mama was part of an association called Benimpuhwe (The Compassionate). This was an association of Rwandan women who lived in exile in Burundi, who held motivational meetings, cultural events, and song and dance lessons. My mother was one of the women who joined early when the association was being formed, and was a dedicated and committed member. It is from Benimpuhwe that she learned how to dance and fell in love with it. Whenever she stood to dance, it was evident to everyone that she wasn't playing. Soon enough, she became quite known as the great light-skinned dancer.

In all dance classes, concerts and events held by Benimpuhwe, my mother was there. Even more, she didn't leave the dance there. She brought dance and Ikinyarwanda with her every time she came home.

The moment I turned five years old, Mama started teaching me how to dance at home. She constantly played Rwandan music cassette tapes on the radio, and we would practice at home. I grew up listening to Muyango, Cecile Kayirebwa, Massamba, Mariya Yohana and other Gakondo icons.

On days that they had practice with the whole group, she would take me, Aggrey and our cousins with her. There, we would meet other girls whose mothers were also dancers in Benimpuhwe, and we would all dance together.

I loved dancing with Mama and I always watched how she swayed her body to the beat of the rhythm given by the drums. That's how I came to honour our dance and appreciate what our culture represented to us.

Mama made sure that she gave me a piece of her passion.

Apart from the dance classes and practice sessions, Benimpuhwe also organized so many concerts, to entertain and motivate Rwandans living in exile, and Mama made sure we never missed them either.

When the liberation struggle began, Benimpuhwe and other Rwandan cultural associations rose to the occasion and started performing to raise funds to send to the front. Mama was one of the leaders in this movement. She did not perform only in Bujumbura, but also in bigger events in Kampala, Uganda, on multiple occasions. As if those efforts were not enough, she went as far as going to the battlefront with some other women to see for themselves what Inkotanyi were doing, and to offer their support.

Laurette Kantengwa was a passionate human being, so whatever she was involved in, she was wholeheartedly involved. She was my model when it came to patriotism. The love and passion that she had for Rwanda, the joy that she unmistakably had when it came to supporting Rwanda and any initiative that pushed for the development of our land, will forever inspire me to dream big and dream for the land of a thousand hills.

Mama, as part of the Benimpuhwe association dances at the front, in one of the fundraising concerts held in Lugogo, Kampala.

Papa, the Intellectual

As we adjusted to our new life in Kampala, Papa worked for UNICEF and on occasion worked at Mulago Hospital in Kampala. His background was in Laboratory engineering and this gave him so many opportunities, amongst which was the capacity to offer his family a very comfortable life in the difficult times that Rwandans were traversing.

Papa was a man for science. From a young age, he always told me to study hard and excel. In his mind, the best career fitting for his daughter was one in the medical field.

Papa pushed for academic excellence. It was either that or nothing really. Performing poorly at school disappointed him so much that his silence in the week following our academic results, was deafening.

Most evenings at home, Papa would do school home works with me, and his strength was in Mathematics. He was the best coach when it came to Mathematics and Sciences.

Papa, during a training at the UNICEF in Djibouti where he worked as the HIV & AIDS Project Officer.

Papa the intellectual was and still is a perfectionist. When it came to excellence in school, he taught me early on that there was no point doing something halfway, or half baked. There was no room for less that 100%.

My early memories of my father were those of him travelling to France in the early 1990s for trainings in his field. It felt wonderful to have a father, not only capable but also exposed because of his intellectual capacity. To this date, though proudly Rwandan and Kinyarwanda speakers, it still gives me joy that we have meaningful conversations and debates on complex matters in English.

Memories of Sheraton Hotel

Some of my best childhood memories were made on Sundays. Some of the greatest life lessons that Papa taught me were during the time that we spent together every after Sunday service.

Every Sunday, we would go to the All Saints Cathedral in Nakasero and after service, he would take us out to the Sheraton Hotel in Kampala.

We would go to the restaurant in the hotel, order tea first and lunch later, then he would proceed to ask us what we had learnt in the Sunday school and how we thought it could be applied to everyday life. During those lunches, he taught us not to lie, not to trick or scheme and to always seek to be honest and authentic. On those lunches, Papa indirectly taught us fine dining at a tender age.

When we had these family moments at the Sheraton, Papa made sure he taught us values such as honesty, love, support and the value of expressing our minds.

Creating memories with a child doesn't necessarily mean doing something grand as having lunch every Sunday at the Sheraton Hotel but the intentionality, consistency and holding meaningful conversations when a parent spends quality time with the child is what lasts in their minds and hearts.

The Sheraton Hotel was somewhat our secret place with Papa every Sunday but it was also his way of creating lasting memories with us and giving us the tool kit that we would need in this life.

He spoiled me

In Kampala, I attended the Buganda Road Primary school for a year or two. One of the rules of the school was that we were to have lunch at the school. Our lunch was often beans and maize "posho". I didn't have this lunch for so long though. I tried the posho lunch for the first three days, got sick and Papa wasn't having it any longer. He informed the school administration that I wasn't going to be having lunch at school.

Every single day, David our driver would drive to my school with a home cooked meal by Mama and I would sit in the back seat and comfortably eat my lunch and then return to school for the afternoon classes.

David would then drive back home with my little brother who only studied a half day. In the evening, David would pick me and then pick Papa and we would set off for home.

Come to think of it, I was a spoiled daddy's girl and I thoroughly enjoyed it. I mean, if blessed to have a loving father, who wouldn't? Being a daddy's girl however didn't serve me well when he would travel abroad. It was well known that whenever he travelled, I would fall sick, only to recover when he landed back. I would have separation anxiety and get sick in his absence. This phenomenon went on until one of his friends advised him to give me some of his t-shirts to wear in his absence. When he did this, I never got sick again when he travelled.

His passion for Education

Studying in Uganda was very different from studying in Burundi. I had to completely switch from the Francophone system to the Anglophone system, take on the rigorous workload that we were given at school and in a foreign language. It was not easy at all.

At some point, Papa got us a tutor to assist us with school work because we were lagging behind.

After the first term, I had adapted and everything sailed smoothly from then on. Papa's reasoning was; "It was either excellence or not" and for that, he was willing to do whatever it took to set us on the right path academically.

Freedom of Expression

My parents were the realest people that I knew. If Papa was angry, he wouldn't attempt to hide it. If mom was happy, her laugh would reverberate in the whole house and if she wasn't happy, best believe that she was going to show that to you. As such, I was told that, from the moment that I could learn to talk, I couldn't keep quiet and along with that came my way of thinking out loud. I was encouraged to be expressive and authentic. Truth was the order of the day in our home.

Fortunately, though loud and unfiltered, I was never silenced. Well, on some occasions I would be too much to handle because I would ask too many questions but despite it all, Papa made sure that I had the freedom to share what I thought.

There was so much freedom in our house that my parents could pause and actually ask us, the children, what we thought.

I was very young but from a tender age, I was shown that my thoughts mattered. This definitely made me quite outspoken.

I was never shy when it came to talking. Yes, I could feel uncomfortable at times, but I was never shy.

In most cases, Mama always said that I was too old for my age and that's why I always had so much to say that was beyond my years. Looking back, being the firstborn and a daughter also contributed to this. I was told from an early age that I had to be responsible and to think like a grown-up. So, I was raised in an advanced way beyond my age.

It was quite confusing, but I benefited tremendously from this upbringing in many ways.

A Tomboy among boys

Over the years, one thing has never left me. Yes, I have grown and adapted as a woman but I have never lost the tomboy streak. Understandably so, I was raised with two of my brothers; played boy games, street soccer to be precise, and yes believe it. I loved and played street soccer with my brothers and their friends on the road before our house in Bibare. My brothers Aggrey and Patrick Mpfizi fed that streak a lot. To this date, we still talk like brothers, though the big sister slash mother figure that I am dominates. My father and brothers have influenced the way I relate with men. It's always easy. I grew up around boys and with a close and deep connection to my father, these relationship dynamics helped my relationships with men.

Work starts early

During the long holidays after my middle high school education (Tronc-Commun) at La Colombière High School, Mama got me a part time job at the MTN Rwanda Centre at "Kwa Rwahama," a well-known building on the road to Kimironko, in Kigali.

At the time, MTN Rwanda was still mass printing talk time voucher cards that needed price tags and they were looking for young people to do that work for three months.

Mama, being good at networking, she managed to get me my first job at the MTN for three months. I was fifteen years old when I started got my first job.

It was a very foreign concept back then, to get a teenage daughter to work when she still had her parents alive and capable to sustain her. Unbeknown to her, however, she taught me hard work early. I remember her telling me, "Do not be a lazy girl, you have to learn to work and work hard. Your life will depend on it!" MTN facilitated her in the pursuit of teaching me the benefits of working hard. We would start work at 8 o'clock in the morning and finish at 4 o'clock in the afternoon. From the moment that we got in those store rooms, our supervisor would give each one of us a batch of cards and price tag stickers to put on those cards for the whole day.

You needed to be focused and disciplined to ensure that you finished your batch on time.

This experience taught me a lot when it comes to work ethics and am forever grateful to Mama and that holiday initiative that MTN Rwanda extended to us when were still young. At that tender age, I learnt that one has to work to gain a living.

At the end of the month, I got my salary. I don't know if I should call it a salary but I got paid eighty thousand Rwandan francs and I was over the moon!

I remember taking the money at home and asking my parents what to do with it and they both smiled. Papa, proudly said, "Barbara, hard work pays off. You can spend that money on yourself," to which Mama jumped in and said, "Give me a little bit and contribute to some expenses in the house."

I did give Mama ten thousand, paid my tithe at the church and in the rest, I bought some sweets for my brothers and bought some clothes for myself. It felt good to "eat" the fruit of my labor.

Over the years, this great lesson on work and money taught me invaluable ethics such as responsibility, contentment and management of what I have worked for.

A child is a canvas for art and the first artists to paint on it are the parents. The creativity, art and skill that those parents put on that canvas determine the worth that that piece will have in the gallery of life. If the parents invest in the fine paint, the skill and the creativity necessary to paint a masterpiece, truly, that piece will be sold to the highest bidder.

A child is shaped first and foremost by their parents or whoever raises them. I was privileged to be raised by parents who gave me a voice, pushed me to pursue more in life and always seek to be a blessing to people.

When I reminisce about my childhood, I often tell myself, "God placed me in the right hands that equipped me to become who I am today."

Dear reader, while I humbly share these childhood experiences with you, I do recognize that many may not have been privileged to be raised by their parents and it greatly affected their lives, others may not have had present and intentional parents, and for that I am so sorry.

On the other side of the coin however, allow me to encourage you by saying this; you could be a different storyline from the one in your upbringing and my wish for you is that you will resolve to giving better to your children, shaping them to become forces to reckon with. Godspeed!

Chapter Two

Shaped By Religion

Growing up, I was raised to believe that Sunday was a special day, a day when we would go to church, pray to the all-powerful God and hope for a better life. I was raised to understand the need for God in our everyday lives, as He was portrayed to me as an all-powerful being that we could ask for anything and get it because He loved children. On so many occasions, Papa would tell me, "Barbara, pray. God will always answer your prayers because He loves children very much," thus, I grew to love praying and getting to know Him better.

My father was a protestant who grew up in a strict Lutheran household, and my mother was a Catholic. They were both not strictly-adhering Christians, but they had the basics in check. They made sure we prayed before going to bed or before eating, and that we knew if we believed in God, we would be in good standing with Him.

Despite being of different denominations, they established that the essential for us was our introduction to God, faith and prayer. To them, the rest, we would figure out as we grew up.

Christ was born in Bethlehem

At the time we lived in Kampala, Uganda, we attended the All-Saints Cathedral. Since Mama didn't speak English, she couldn't attend any mass in Kampala. Because of that, the common understanding that my parents had of exposing Aggrey and I to both denominations did not really work out, and that's how we ended up only going to the All Saints Cathedral with Papa every Sunday. There, we learned so many fascinating Bible stories and hymns.

During these Sundays, there was a particular English song I easily learned by heart, that talked about how Christ was born in Bethlehem. I didn't fully comprehend the concepts and pillars of the Christian faith such as the meaning behind the nativity story but I sang this song for days like it was the only English song ever composed. Even though I didn't have the angelic voice, Christ was born in Bethlehem is the first Christian song that I learnt and the one that I enjoyed most. Plus, every guest who would come at home, I would offer to sing it for them.

One Friday evening, Papa and Mama took us out to a bar in Kabalagala. It was a strip lined with countless bars where people drank, ate grilled chicken and danced on the road. They enjoyed the company of fellow Rwandans who hung out there, with whom they'd reminisce about their past and share their hopes for Rwanda. I don't know why our parents took us there, but we loved it. It was somewhat an occasional family habit for spending time together and having fun. They loved the music, we loved the food. It was a great combination.

A renowned Rwandan artist, Dede Majoro, used to perform live, singing Kinyarwanda, Swahili and English songs there, and he always had the people on their feet, dancing. One particular evening, Dede asked the audience if there was anyone who wanted him to sing a special song, and Papa looked at me and told me, "You know, you can sing Christ was born in Bethlehem."

Taken by surprise, and scared by what I had just heard, I told him that there were so many people and that I couldn't stand in front of them and sing. He insisted, saying that he was sure I could do it. Still trying to convince him that I couldn't sing, hc raised his hand and called, "Dede," out loud. "My daughter has a special song that she would like to perform!"

O God!

Dede walked up to us, excited and a little tipsy. He held my hand, took me onto the stage and told the crowd, "This young lady called Barbara has a song for you all. Please pay attention to her and give her a round of applause after she's done," then handed me the microphone.

Singing Christ was born in Bethlehem in a bar, late at night, people drunk, I mean, thinking about it now...that was insane! As I sang, the whole place was dead quiet. It was such a surreal moment. I felt a presence that I had never felt before covering me as I sang. I couldn't make sense of it, but I knew that something weird had just happened to me. In a bar full of drunken adults looking at me and wondering why I had to sing Christ, of all people, there, I preached my first sermon in a song.

Finding God as a teenager & Receiving Christ

After we had moved to Kigali, we went to church on Sundays as usual, except this time it was either with Mama for a Catholic mass or with Papa at the Eglise Presbytérienne du Rwanda in Kiyovu. Recitals in the Catholic Church were quite a challenge for us though, so on most occasions, we opted for Papa's church because we preferred their more vibrant songs.

Sunday church service was a way of refreshing ourselves and getting ready for the week ahead.

After church, we would head home to a delicious lunch that Mama would have cooked after attending her mass. We would have lunch, take a nap and wake up to organize our school work for the upcoming week.

From a young age, I had a somewhat childish relationship with God, but nothing like what I was about to have as a teenager.

One long, dragging week, my family was struck by a crisis that left me so shaken and afraid. It was during that week that I made the most important prayer of my life. It was simple, silent, not led by any pastor, but by God alone.

I prayed, "God, I need you in my life. I need you to come lead me and keep me safe. I welcome you. Come and be my God every day." At the end of it, I was immediately overcome by a sense of peace and comfort. I didn't know where it came from but one thing was for sure…I was going to be fine. From that day, I was convicted that whenever I cried for help from above, I would always get it. And indeed, I always did.

I made my personal and meaningful connection with God for the first time in my life that day.

From then on, I recognized that God was the most consistent and most reliable being that could walk with me through the different storms of life, and I resolved to always give Him the trust that He was worthy of.

Receiving Christ again...and again

Before you judge me, let me just say that I am not the only believer who has received Christ more than once. The church (Église Presbytérienne du Rwanda) in Sonatubes, Kicukiro, where Papa used to take us on occasions when driving to the Kiyovu one was hard, was more than a Protestant church. I would say that it had a Pentecostal spice to it, now that I know much more about the different denominations.

Every time the pastor finished preaching, he would make the altar call, and guess who went there every single time. Me! I received Christ at least three more times until the ushers who would come to know me told me that God had heard my prayer the first time, that since the first day that I invited Him in my heart, that prayer had been answered and it was enough. They told me that the next step for me was to focus on growing in the knowledge of who God was, and for this to happen, I was going to need to buy a Bible to study more about God.

I loved the church sermons probably more than the praise and worship. I loved how the pastors knew what they were talking about, and from where I sat in the pews, it seemed to me that the Bible was the magical book from which they got all the words they told us. The sermons added something of value to me. I couldn't define it, but I just knew I was a different person every time I left church.

One Sunday, on my way outside the church building after service, I noticed ushers who were selling Bibles and I walked to them and asked them how much they cost. "Two thousand Rwandan francs," they told me, and I knew what I had to do. I had to get Mama to buy me one, and she couldn't refuse. Going back home that day, I couldn't contain my anticipation to give Mama my request.

Open to the Word

At home, lunch was ready, but I immediately and directly asked Mama after hugging her, "Mama, can I have two thousand? I really, really want a Bible, and that's how much they cost at the church." She smiled and told me, "Remind me on Saturday evening and I will give it to you to buy your Bible on Sunday."

I counted the days, but Saturday evening couldn't come any sooner. When it finally did, I reminded Mama of her promise and she quickly obliged, and asked me to get her handbag and gave me the money. Sunday morning, I was up and ready for church early, and I went straight to buy my Bible as soon as we got there.

Once in church, I couldn't wait for the sermon. I was finally going to open my brand new Bible and read along with the adults. The only challenge I had was that I didn't know how to locate what we were supposed to be reading. Fortunately, the pastor knew that some people in the congregation were in the same predicament as me, and he directed us to the table of contents on the first pages.

From that Sunday onwards, each time we attended church, I always carried my prized possession with pride and honor. I paid attention to what the pastor would be teaching and once I got home, I would devote time to re-read the Scripture and try to think about what the pastor taught during service. Reading the Bible soon became my escape into another world that I was unfamiliar with; a world of great imagination, possibilities, miracles and greatness, and yes, great stories. I loved the stories!

I fell more in love with this big book every time I devoted myself to reading it. In the evenings, I would come from school, take a shower and quickly finish my homework to spare at least one hour in my Bible before bedtime. That hour in the evening was very precious to me. I explored the Bible, with no given structure, reading it until I felt sleepy.

On many occasions my parents wondered where I got this habit, since we were not that religious. Yes, we went to church on Sundays, but we were not an everyday Bible reading family. Papa once told me that he wasn't surprised that I was this attached to the Bible, since my paternal grandfather was an elder in the Lutheran Church and could never part ways with his Bible. He believed that I probably got that from my grandfather. Whichever way my parents defined that phase of my life, it didn't bother me. It instead made me love the letters in that dark leather covered book even more.

Not until many years down the road did I understand why I had that fire for God's Word, and the impact that those letters had on my soul became even more undeniable.

The Cave

Sometime in 1998, we had to move from the house we had grown to love so much in Niboye. The landlady wanted it back. Papa and Mama searched for and found another house for us to live in, in Bibare, Remera, a suburb of Kigali. We moved there and a few months later, my parents got a mortgage and bought that piece of land, which had two houses built on it. It belonged to close family friends and so it felt like home from the beginning. We gained extended cousins, sisters, brothers, aunties, uncles, people I still consider as family today.

That was our new home, and we would never go through the hassle of packing our bags and moving from house to house again. That's where I grew up as a young girl. That's where most of my teenage memories come from. That's where I lived when I learnt so many life lessons that I cherish till this day.

In 1999, a new church movement overtook the whole country. It was known as the Abarokore (The Born Again) movement. Initially, I didn't really know much about them. I came to know them through the unease that my parents felt about my obsession with my Bible.

"Barbara, you can read your Bible, go to the Protestant church at Sonatubes, but I will never allow you to join Abarokore," Papa expressed one evening. "They brainwash people's minds and turn them into blind followers, and that is not our religion. Your only options are the Catholic church or the Protestant church…no other church is allowed in this household."

Little did he know what he had done in saying those words, and what was about to happen. By saying this statement, Papa actually got me so curious that I wanted to try out attending a service of Abarokore. His stand on that movement made me wonder; "What is so wrong about these people that Papa would be so adamant about them?"

One of the older "cousins" that I had gained called Clarisse who we nicknamed Dudu, had started attending a new born again church with her sisters and neighborhood friends, at a place called The Cave. It was a small basement in one of the few flats on the road in Remera to Sonatubes, which accommodated around one hundred people inside and a few tens outside.

Clarisse and Chantal, also next-door neighbors, had joined this movement and caught their guardians' attention. One weekend, Clarisse's uncle and auntie came over to visit and shared their concerns with my parents, telling them that this new movement was taking young people and brainwashing them, but at least had some positivity about it. The young people who joined the movement tended to be well mannered and calmer than their peers.

By calm, they meant that they didn't drink, smoke or go to the club every weekend. To some extent, this gave some reassurance to my parents.

As they were sharing this, they mentioned that one of their nephews, Maurice, who we nicknamed Dede, had completely turned his life around after giving his life to Christ, and was no longer partying a lot. With that trust, I believe that my parents' hearts were open to me going for a church service at The Cave.

One Saturday evening, weeks after that conversation, Clarisse came over to our house and asked my parents for permission to take me there. They accepted and without knowing it, set me off on a journey that has led me to who I am today. The following Sunday morning, we went and attended my first service at The Cave.

Reaching the entrance, two women met and greeted us with beaming smiles, "Yesu ashimwe (Praise Jesus)," to which Clarisse responded with, "Ahimbazwe (Praise Him)" As we entered, I heard vibrant music being played and people singing along to songs I didn't know but loved instantly once we took our seats.

The atmosphere in that tiny hall was electric, celebratory and intense. I stood to clap my hands along with everyone else, and I felt goosebumps spread all over my arms. It was rare for me to feel that way. I probably did on a few occasions in my room when I would read my Bible for more than one hour, but it wasn't quite the same feeling. I felt the presence of someone I couldn't see.

Soon, the music stopped and a man stood up to tell us what was next. He made the church announcements, which were mostly about weekly services, prayer meetings and where and when those who needed special counselling sessions could get them. Shortly after, he asked the ushers to collect offerings while the music band played a softer tone. As we finished with the collection of offerings, he led us in a short prayer to receive the Word of God, which I figured to be the sermon.

Introducing the preacher, he said, "Dear brothers and sisters, allow me to welcome our senior pastor, Pastor Paul Gitwaza, to come and give us what the Lord has placed on his heart." He hadn't finished introducing the pastor when everyone in the hall had stood on their feet, clapping their hands and whistling to welcome him. This was odd for me, given that this wasn't how we did it in our Protestant Church or even in the Catholic mass, but I was curious to know exactly what was so special about this pastor that everyone welcomed him in this way.

Pastor Paul was a lean, dark and tall man with an afro and a big smile. He took the microphone and greeted the cheering congregation. He then waited for the congregation to calm down before asking for an acoustic guitar, and started singing.

As he sang, we all connected to a presence in that tiny hall, and I could literally feel my heart open up and sense the power. After his song, Pastor Paul preached a sermon about living with Jesus as a friend. This preacher had a way of materialising Scripture in a way that I had never experienced before. I felt Jesus in that tiny room, touching each of our souls. It's at that moment that I knew that this was the church I wanted to attend every Sunday.

A Preacher in the making

My first three years of high school were at La Colombière High School. It was also during the last year that my relationship with the Lord deepened, that I found myself attracted to like-minded colleagues.

Every break time, we would find ourselves in small groups, discussing Scripture or sharing personal testimonies of what God was doing in our lives. As young believers, the thirty minute breaks were precious to us, since those who were grown enough to attend weekly church services would come and share with us what they would have learned at church, and that would build our faith.

At some point, we decided that sharing the Word of God amongst ourselves wasn't enough. We needed to share Christ with our classmates, and so we did. We would disperse and approach small groups of students and ask them if we would share with them the good news of Christ.

At first, we were the odd group of Abarokore to them, but then they got used to us and would listen politely or tell us that they were still thinking about what we told them the previous week. We were on a mission to get people to receive Christ as their Lord and Savior and if they didn't, we would keep coming back until they either asked us to stop, or they heard our messages.

Eventually, this activity became unwelcome to some students and they reported us to the Headmaster, Mr. Génade. He was a very strict and focused gentleman, and no one wanted to get on his wrong side. On one end of the spectrum, there were students who were on fire and burning with zeal after receiving Christ, and on the other end there was the school Headmaster who didn't want any religious activities going on during school hours.

Mr. Génade once found me quietly preaching to a small group of girls who were in Senior One, and took me aside for the "talk." He looked me square in the eyes and said, "Barbara, I understand your enthusiasm for sharing your belief, but it is not allowed on school grounds. So, before it gets too bad, please stop. The next time I catch you telling students about faith related stories, I will have to suspend you."

Talk about being shaken to silence. I wasn't going to have my parents come to the school because of my new found faith and a "brainwashed" version of Barbara that they were not used to, so I started thinking of other ways to preach without really preaching, and I had to make sure that I never got suspended. You might be wondering why I insisted on breaking the school regulations. I frankly didn't know why. I just knew that I had to share Christ.

One evening, during my Bible study at home, I took some notes on a piece of paper and found it quite interesting. I thought to myself, "If I print many copies of my notes and share them with other students, I would still be sharing Christ without really rallying students during recess hours." The next morning, I gave that piece of paper to my Mama to assist me with making thirty copies, which she gladly obliged.

She was less strict, compared to Papa who didn't want me to overwhelm myself by mixing school with other "unnecessary" activities. As long as I brought in the grades, she was fine.

That evening, she brought the copies and handed them to me, and before going to bed, I took a pair of scissors and cut them to size, and kept them in my bag.

The next day when I went to school, the plan was to give them to students after class on our way out, heading home from school. As we were going outside the school compound, I stood outside the gate and randomly gave those papers to students. I did this for the amount of times that Mama was willing to make copies for me in a week. I did this for a month, before I had to stop completely.

Mr. Genade found out about it, and this time called my parents and told them to warn me because it was getting out of hand and heading to a suspension. One evening, my parents sat me down and told me that I was clearly brainwashed and they were not having it anymore. I was to stop preaching or handing out tracts. As a matter of fact, I was not going to attend The Cave anymore, since it "fueled my madness." This suspension was tougher on me than any other disciplinary measures ever taken on me.

Today, as a parent myself, and as I reflect on that season of my youth, I think that they did the best they could to shield me as a child whose spirituality had overtaken her life. I also think that my zeal, which is so common in new believers, combined with adolescence and immaturity, got me so fired up that my parents had to keep a close eye on me.

In hindsight however, God was preparing me for bigger things and with His infinite wisdom, used my passion and drive to mold me into His servant.

Winner Youth

When my parents suspended all church related activities for me, another group of young believers became my place of fellowship. This group called Winner Youth was a youth ministry growing in the early 2000s in Kigali, and it brought so many young people from different churches together for prayer and sharing the Word.

I first came into contact with this group one Saturday afternoon when I went to visit a neighborhood and school friend, Grace who we nicknamed Finotte. She was a friend I used to ride on the same school bus and also attend church with. At this point, Authentic Word Ministries, which met at The Cave, had birthed a church called Zion Temple and had moved across the street to a larger open space that could seat at least two thousand people. Finotte's whole family had been converted and was attending Zion Temple. And as a result, they would host small group prayers at their home on different days.

Every Saturday afternoon, Winner Youth would gather as a cell at their house, bringing together tens of youths in that fellowship. On the day I met the Winner Youth, I totally felt akin to them. They were young people who shared my faith, zeal and passion for Christ. I met some great souls in that group that are still my friends to this day.

Peer mentorship was one of the tools that Winner Youth used in keeping us engaged in our walk with the Lord and in ministry, at the same time allowing us to be young and focused. It's in the Winner Youth meetings that I was baptized in the Spirit, spoke in tongues for the first time, learned to speak in a group of people, and it is also there that I learned to interpret for a preacher.

My Christian background set me on a path of faith. From a tender age to adulthood, I have seen the benefits of believing in God through His Son Jesus Christ, not giving up on hope and overcoming fear for the future. I was shaped by faith in the sense that, throughout my life, I have always known that God would come through for me. Faith has been my solid anchor and His Word has indeed served as the manual for my life.

Being exposed as a child to faith tuned my world view to one which I attribute how I perceive life and beyond. Faith will do that to you. Faith in God will take away the fear and empower you for the future.

In the cases where we focus on religion, I believe that we are misguided. Rather, focusing on faith is the best thing, not religion and certainly not in our religious differences.

Chapter Three

Shaped By Independence

In the late nineties, towards the early years of the new century, so many families in Kigali were using all their resources to find ways to send their children to Europe and North America for a better life and a better education than what was available in Rwanda. In our neighborhood in Bibare, a suburb in Kigali, most families sent their teenagers outside the country too, except for my family and our immediate neighbors.

We didn't have direct relatives living in the West and my parents were not ready to send me to live with extended family members just for the sake of it. They believed, and rightly so, that I was too young to go and live so far and so disconnected from what I still needed from our family setting. So, I stayed put, despite the pressure and fear of missing out on what my peers were experiencing. I finished my middle high school education at La Colombière High School, and started my Higher Advanced Courses (HAC) level at Lycée de Kigali specializing in Maths and Physics. Shortly after, I transitioned to the Biology and Chemistry specialization and was set to give it my best, driven by Papa's dream of me becoming a doctor.

But in early 2002, life took me and my family off script and presented a once in a lifetime opportunity that would prove to be a wild ride.

Uwase

One evening, Papa came back home so excited like he'd won the lottery. He sat us down, showed us a big envelope and said, "I have a great surprise for you." I wondered what surprise he had that had him that happy. He pulled some papers that he had clearly printed photos on from his office printer. He looked at them before handing them to me and saying, "Barbara, meet Maryan. She is your sister."

"What? We have a sister? How? Since when?" Too many questions ran through my mind but quickly vanished. The beauty of this new sister of mine was something to behold that the questions could come back later.

Maryan, who Papa later named Uwase, was born when he was in college.

Her mother was a Somali woman that he had met in Dar-es-Salaam. Uwase was his first born, eight years older than me. Looking at her photos, I couldn't help but notice that she got the best of both parents in her genes. I didn't know her mother but I could tell that she had Papa's long legs and hands.

Very tall, light skinned and slender, she looked like a model. Came to find out later that she had actually modeled for some time.

Maryan lived in London, England and had been tirelessly looking for her father for so many years, until that day when she got Papa's number, and called and had one of the most memorable phone conversations of her life with him. She wanted to know everything there was to know about Papa, Mama, us, our culture, our lives, and Rwanda.

I could understand her drive in connecting with all of us at a go. There was so much about us that was a part of who she was, and there was so much she had missed out on that she wanted to learn. This newly discovered father-daughter relationship took off on a high speed, and in less than six months, Papa had gone to London to meet Maryan.

Their reunion was one for the books.

Maryan wanted to connect with her siblings too and during Papa's trip to London she requested that I join her and stay with her there. When Papa travelled back home, he shared the gifts and letters that she had sent us before breaking the news to us with excitement.

"Barbara, looks like you are finally getting your big break. Maryan is excited and looking forward to welcoming and hosting you in London!"

Culture Shock

The great news was met with uncertainty, especially from my mother. Yes, I really wanted to go and live in Europe, but going at such a young age and with blind faith to live with a newly discovered sibling was far-fetched to Mama.

We'd lived different lives, had different backgrounds and upbringings, and had a big age difference that would set each of us on the path of a cultural shock on an already nonexistent relationship. However, God had His hand in this whole setup, and Papa ended up convincing Mama that sending me to my sister was a greater arrangement than me going to live simply anywhere.

In August 2002, with tears flowing, I bid farewell to my whole family and friends and travelled to Europe with Mama. We first went to Belgium where we stayed with my aunties for a week.

From there, leaving Mama behind, I crossed over to England with one of my aunties who was more familiar with the UK.

We travelled by Coach for the whole night for what seemed like an endless drive, and arrived in the morning at Waterloo Station in Central London.

Arriving at the station, my aunt went to a nearby callbox and called Maryan to tell her that we had arrived safely. Maryan told us she'd be on her way and that it would take her at least an hour or so to get to us from where she lived in East London. We then decided to go to a nearby coffee shop for some breakfast as we waited for her. My aunt probably felt that I was going to need a last minute pep talk, so she started adding more to the talks that we had already had back at her house with Mama.

She warmly looked at me and said, "Barbara, you are still so young and Europe is a very difficult place to live. Please keep praying and stay focused. Study hard, pass well and make your parents proud. Do not expect much from people, because you might be disappointed. Here, your father, mother and brothers will not be around to encourage you every single day, so you are all you got and I know that you will manage so well. Just remain focused as a Christian, and you will survive."

In about an hour, Maryan reached us, excited and so happy to see us. She hugged us and carried my luggage as we walked towards the underground station. We were both happy to finally meet, but we didn't know what to talk about. She kept asking me about Papa, Mama and the other kids, and I responded to all her questions with a smile.

Naturally, I am an extrovert, and a sanguine, but I have a tendency of going all quiet when I haven't really known someone. I am the kind that will live in a shell until I know a person well enough to feel safe before I come out. But once out, rest assured that I will be the life of the party every day!

So, on that first day that I met my sister, I would say that I was comfortably seated in my shell, studying my new sister, environment and new life that was awaiting me in this foreign land. It would be a while before I came out from my familiar shell.

We soon arrived at her house and she welcomed us to the living room, and offered us some juice and snacks while she put our bags in the guest room. She was so hospitable and determined to make us comfortable. I found her endearing. As we sat in the living room, she switched on the TV for us, and went to cook us a proper meal. I could tell that this unexpected blessing in our family was going to teach me so many life lessons.

After a few days, my aunt returned to Belgium and I stayed with Maryan for a few months before moving out to start life on my own.

Within the first week, I could tell that my sister and I were different, but also similar in ways we probably couldn't tell just yet. Maryan came from a Muslim background and I came from a Christian one. This difference was so apparent in that most of her culture, habits and mannerisms were tied to that background, whereas mine were a mixture of my Rwandan upbringing, culture and belief system. One thing that was a must for me however, was living in harmony and peace with her. I made it a point that I would never have a misunderstanding with her because I couldn't blame either one of us for the differences in our upbringings, which we had never asked for in the first place.

On most days while living with her, when I wasn't battling nostalgia and depression from experiencing a shift that I hadn't anticipated and was too young to fully comprehend, I was busy trying to help with chores and forge a relationship that could benefit both of us.

It was not an easy entry into this new life away from home in a foreign continent with a new sister, and I think that it wasn't easy for her either.

Maryan had a gaping hole in her heart caused by not being raised by her father, and I was on the other side missing the father that she never knew. I think that when she looked at me, she saw me as a spoiled daughter, something that she had never had the privilege to have, and when I looked at her, I didn't know how to connect to her and her past. But we had to meet somewhere, somehow. We did have our differences, but I am grateful to her for being wise and mindful that our relationship would grow with much effort over time.

While staying in her East London apartment, I learned so much from my Somali sister. I learned how to cook. Goodness she is a gifted cook!!!! She taught me the corners and places in London, where to get basic needs, and how to survive on a low budget in the big city.

In her own way, Maryan prepared me so well for living independently in London, that by the time I moved out, I wasn't totally lost. I was ready… or at least, I thought I was.

Papa with his daughters; Barbara and Maryan M. Uwase.

Margaret Cassidy House

Margaret Cassidy House, my home for two years when I had just moved to London, UK.

From our cultural standpoint, no one really prepares a teenage daughter to move out of the family home to go and live alone. It is unheard of. A daughter is supposed to move out of the family home when she is going to get married. Any time before then is pretty much rebellious or "Western," and it is conceived as a major 'faux pas' for the parents. Society will judge them as careless and insensitive parents for exposing a girl to the wild, outside the comfort and protection of the family home.

It is supposed that she is at risk of meeting the wrong kind of friends, get in a relationship with a boy, have sex, get pregnant before marriage and taint the "perfect" family name. So, with that mindset, daughters, moreover teenagers are meant to stay under the protective supervision of the parents, guardians or older siblings.

This was not my trajectory as an adolescent. I separated from my beloved parents in the prime of my teenage years and went to live in England, in the United Kingdom. In a short time, I also had to move from my sister's house because it was time I settled in my own life. And to do that, I had to do what everyone else in my predicament was doing.

Telling another story

A great number of youths from Africa who migrate to the West for various reasons, undergo the baptism of hardship through the seeking of asylum in these foreign countries.

In early spring of 2002, I was one of those who set herself on that unprecedented path. To do that, I had to meticulously present my reasons for claiming asylum, and they had to be convincing enough for me to not be deported back to Africa.

The logic in this is that once you manage to get accepted in the system, you are given opportunities to study in some of the best education systems in the world, the employment opportunities are a lot, and there are more possibilities to help you financially take care of your family back home.

The reasons that I came up with were regular, ones that any sixteen year old could come up with, but overall, I presume that I did well since those reasons granted me two years in the system, until I was no longer a minor and was set to defend my reasons for wanting to stay in the UK.

When I claimed that I was seeking asylum as a refugee at Heathrow Airport, being a minor, I was taken to the closest shelter for minors called Margaret Cassidy House, by a social worker. Further processing would be done at the Home Office in Croydon, South London. For that evening, I would just be taken in to wait for my appointment.

It must have been at around ten o'clock in the night when I and the social worker entered that building. The security officer, Steve, kindly welcomed me. He was a slightly elderly English man, probably in his fifties, medium height with some grey hair, and he seemed quite accustomed to receiving minors from the Immigration Office. He handled my accommodation file and gave me some tea to drink. It was a typical cold, windy night in London, and I appreciated something warm in my body after a long afternoon and evening.

After completing my registration, Steve took us to my room, gave us the instructions pertaining to staying in that residence and left. My social worker showed me the warm clothes that had been donated to assist the young refugees during the upcoming winter and then gave me food vouchers to use for meals at the nearest local McDonald's before I could receive my weekly income support. She then gave me her business card and informed me that I would have to go to the Uxbridge Council in the morning for further social services processing and for assistance on settling as a minor in that part of London. When all was clear enough for me, she wished me a good night and left.

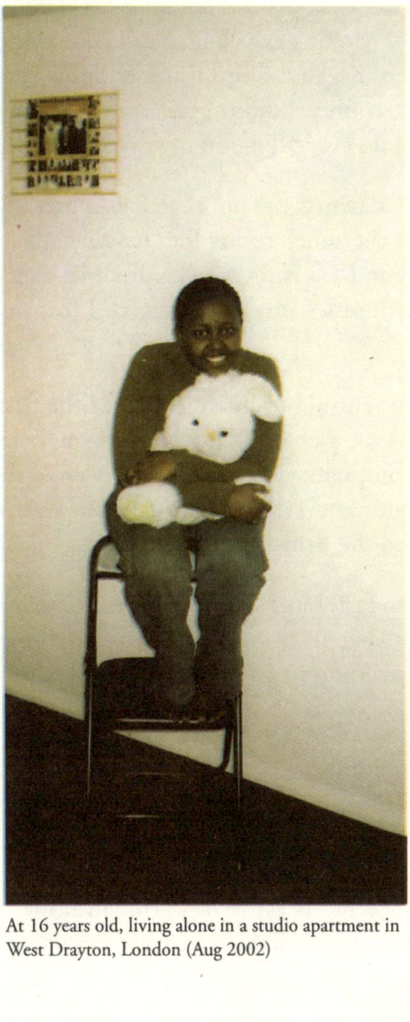

At 16 years old, living alone in a studio apartment in West Drayton, London (Aug 2002)

I was left in that studio apartment alone. I sat on the single bed and all I could do was utter a small prayer; "God, I don't know what my life is going to look like in this place, in this new life, but please keep me safe. Papa and Mama are not here with me. You are all I got. Keep me safe. Keep me sane. This will be hard, but help me survive this life. Amen." I then realized that I was hungry and went out to buy a meal at McDonald's, came back to the house, took a warm shower, had my meal and slept my first night at Margaret Cassidy House.

It would be until two years later, after I turned eighteen, that I'd be moved from Margaret Cassidy House to a nearby shared residential house.

Uxbridge College

The next day, after completing my registration process and being shown what I'd get from the social services, my social worker proceeded to show me a map of the area, highlighting local colleges, banks, shopping malls and supermarkets. She told me to open a bank account for savings, check around the supermarkets and buy food, utensils and all the basics that I would need every day, and told me to go to Uxbridge College and get registered, which I did on that same day.

Prior to this event, I had never heard of banking as a child, besides knowing that my mother worked for the Bank of Kigali; I didn't think or know that children could have their own bank accounts. I didn't even know that as a child, I could get myself a school and do everything on my own.

On that day, at sixteen years old, it dawned on me that I was literally going to lead my own life and it was the shock of my life. It was hard to understand that all I'd have was ME and I was responsible for ME every single day. Right then, in that Council office, my life changed. I lost my childhood innocence.

My time at Uxbridge College was uneventful but interesting. For the first time, I was taking lessons and exams on a computer, which was new to me, coming from a country where computers and the internet were only in government offices, large institutions and cyber cafés. As if that wasn't enough, I also struggled to understand the British accent.

My teachers seemed to always speak so fast, but I was determined to make my parents so proud, so, I was always keen in class. I didn't have anything else to do besides studying, and I was going to give the best of myself to succeed.

To further build my knowledge and command of the English language, I committed to always watch the BBC Morning News bulletin while taking breakfast. I reasoned, these morning presenters would help me learn more about this country and the culture. I also did this to learn more of the language and get familiar with the accent. Because of my commitment and determination, within six months I knew how to navigate the school material, I understood the way things were done in the little town of

Hayes, and that brought me a sense of settlement and security.

Every time I talked to my parents at home, they were worried and unsure if I was handling it all well, but I did my best to reassure them that I was. One of my ways to do so was to always update them on my living situation. This implied that I would call home at least twice a week. I also made it a point to share my academic performance with them on a regular basis. When I sat for exams and got results, I shared them with my parents in their emails. At the time, it was all very costly for me, but it made me feel less lonely and more connected.

Uxbridge College offered me the opportunity to learn so much, acquire a lot of key skills, and this kept me busy and focused. Living as a minor and under the social services care, I also had to keep my social worker informed about my progress, and this kept me on the right track. Since I didn't want to start working and then have less time to focus on my studies, I had a lot of financial challenges, but I knew that there would be time for work and financial stability.

So, the focus then was on finishing college and getting into a great university.

In the early months and even years of my stay in London, depressed, lonely and questioning my whole reason of being there, young, immature, afraid, I was oblivious to the growth that was simultaneously taking place in those months. I had been weaned and definitely not ready for that process but I had begun my journey to self-esteem, confidence, owning my voice and much more.

Independence made me bold, courageous and unwavering. Independence taught me faith in the goodness that an unknown and unpredictable future could hold. Independence developed fighting muscles in my soul; since giving up wasn't an option. For that, I grateful to God and my parents for throwing me in the deep end. On the flip side however, independence in my teenage years took away so much innocence and softness that I grieve sometimes. Nonetheless, I chose to see the good that outweighs the bad in that experience, because, by the time I became settled and used to that life, I knew very well that I could survive anywhere. With God by my side, I could survive anywhere.

Chapter Four

Shaped By Companionship

The first two years living alone in my small studio apartment at Margaret Cassidy House were quite difficult for me. I had moved from being in a family setting to living alone as a teen, and it took a toll on my mental health more than I realized then.

I experienced so many days of deep loneliness, unexplainable sadness and on some occasions, depression. This was due to the fact that I couldn't easily go back home to visit because I didn't have my documents in check, and there was the helplessness that came with not being able to solve that constraint and to solve some problems back home. Thankfully, some people I got to meet on my journey made all this much more bearable.

Assemblée de Dieu

One day, while in the school's computer library sending an email to my mother, a dark skinned, petite-framed young lady walked up to me and introduced herself to me; "Hi. My name is Vanessa. You look Rwandan. Are you Rwandan? I am Rwandan and you look like them"

"Yes I am," I answered with excitement. "My name is Barbara. It's nice to meet you."

As we proceeded with our conversation in Kinyarwanda, Vanessa asked me, "Are you a Christian?" to which I responded with surprise, "Yes I am, but I have failed to find an African church. The only one that I attended was an Ethiopian Pentecostal church, but I never got anything because everything was in Amharic!"

Vanessa reassured me, "Oh, do not worry. There is an Assemblée de Dieu (Assemblies of God) church in Hayes city centre. It is led by a Congolese Pastor and I think that you can easily adapt, compared to the Ethiopian one." We then exchanged our phone numbers and agreed to meet in Hayes the next Sunday, and go to church. I couldn't wait. I had missed going to church, the fellowship, the sermons, the singing, and the people. I had missed church so much.

Sunday came and I was ready by midday, even though the service was to start at two o'clock in the afternoon. I met Vanessa in the city centre as promised and we walked for a few minutes to the building that hosted the church. I was too excited to even think of the language barrier that I was about to encounter. All I knew was that I wanted to be in a church service and I figured that Congolese were closer to Rwandans than Ethiopians, so this was going to work out for me one way or another.

We walked in the sanctuary and were welcomed by praise songs in Lingala, which were so familiar from back home in Zion Temple. I felt at home instantly. That first service was mostly nostalgic for me. It made me miss home and my home church so much.

Once the praise and the announcements were done, the moderator welcomed the preacher to share the sermon. The preacher walked up to the stage to the acclaim of the congregation and I could feel the vibrancy and liveliness I used to feel in my home church back in Rwanda.

The pastor was well aware of the different nationalities in the congregation, so he had a way of meshing French, English and Lingala in his sermon. To me, that was amazing because I could speak French fluently, and it was my first time hearing Lingala being spoken. I knew that in a matter of months I would catch up quickly, and indeed, I did.

After fellowshipping in that church for a month, I asked God to help me understand what would be spoken in Lingala since everything was done in Lingala and I often felt left out, and He did! This miracle only happened to me during the sermon.

Whenever the pastor would speak in Lingala, my spirit had a way of understanding what he would say that by the second month, I stopped asking for an interpreter because I understood pretty much everything. I should note that, when the sermon would be done however, I wouldn't understand much of what these precious people would be saying.

Within two months, I asked the deacons to join the Ushers department, and started ministering in that church. I figured that it was going to be my church, so I had to find a way to give back and help. That would also serve to help me integrate myself better in that community as one of their own. The majority of the congregation was Congolese and as it was their culture, everything was done the Congolese way. So to fit right in, I had to intentionally learn some Lingala through fellow ushers and soon enough, I joined the Intercessors department and spent more time with these brothers and sisters.

They never treated me as a "Rwandan", despite the politics between our countries back home. They welcomed me to their homes, loved me, fed me, and clothed me. In no time, they had become my extended family in West London.

To me, I was finally settling and ready to grow in this foreign yet so welcoming land. I felt I would be fine as long as I had a school to go to, a church to attend, and also good friends by my side.

A Twin and a Sister

At Margaret Cassidy House, I met a Rwandan named Rama Jason. He was the first Rwandan that I had met there, so you can imagine the sense of relief I felt when I met him. Oh, how I had missed talking in Kinyarwanda with fellow Rwandans!

Jay, as we fondly called him, was and still is such a kind soul. He had an amazing sense of humor and always made me feel good about being Rwandan. Some of my fondest memories of him are the Sunday lunches, Saturday dinners, and sometimes church services we would attend together. One day at dinner, we shared our family histories and I asked him his birthday, and to my surprise we shared the same date. Jay looked at me and told me right away, "You are now my twin, and I know that life is not easy here, but I will try to be your brother here." He could tell that the first years were difficult on me so he kept his promise and made it a point to always check on me and reassure me, "Barbara, humura. Tuzabaho neza muri iki gihugu (Barbara, don't worry. We'll live well in this country)." For the entirety of the time I spent in the UK, he was always there for me.

Jay did not only stand as my brother at that time. He also introduced me to a girl named Mnanira Teri, who too quickly became more of a sister than a friend.

Teri was driven, focused and very disciplined. She always pushed me to excel academically. Whenever we would break for holidays, she would always check on me to see if I performed well and if I didn't, she wouldn't be happy. She constantly reminded me, "We are here for a better life, for ourselves and for our families back home, so there is no time to play around. Do not forget that." She passed me the ropes on staying focused while living alone as a young woman in a foreign land where I had no parental supervision.

Teri would cook and invite me and Jason to her house to share meals. Some other days, we would do each other's hair, go grocery shopping together, study together, you mention it. We always had something to do together on the weekend because Teri never passed any opportunity to keep me busy and grounded.

My sister, Teri, and my twin, Jay, both raised me indirectly in my first two years living alone in London. To this day, they check on me. Every 22nd of August, Jay and I celebrate and advise each other, when need be, cheer each other up, and keep our friendship alive. When in Rwanda, they visit my family, bring my children gifts, and they make sure that I remember that distance is nothing but miles…not the end of a relationship.

Teri N. Mnanira, the sister that raised me. Uxbridge, London in 2004.

Rama J, the twin that I didn't know that I needed.

New Cross Family

In South East London, is an area called New Cross, there lived a family that took interest in me and drastically changed my life. I met them at the newly launched Zion Temple, which I had excitedly started attending shortly after it opened in London.

A man named Félin Gakwaya approached me one evening after service, and wanted to know more about my life. He asked me where I lived and what I was studying, and to his surprise, he learn't that I consistently made long commutes to church, despite the financial constraints I had. He looked at me and made one of the most precious offers ever made to me while living in London. "Barbara," he said. "Our home is open for you every weekend. Please come every Friday evening, and leave on Sunday after service. You need a family, and mine will gladly take you in."

Félin lived in New Cross, London with his wife, Dadali Josée Gakwaya. They were a young couple, newly-wed and expecting their first born daughter. These were people who didn't know me or my family personally. We had just met in church and they took me in without hesitation.

Now, this family wasn't as small as I had initially thought. Félin's siblings, Patel and Chantal "Bobette" Gakwaya lived nearby but spent most of their time at their house, as well as Josée's sister, Sifa, who also lived near Central London.

Every weekend, we would all come to New Cross, have tea and then head for evening prayers and fellowship at the residence of a man known as Brother Richard Budigoma. After prayers, we would go back to Félin's house for the rest of the weekend.

Josée created such a safe environment for all of us that we felt at home. She gracefully cooked our meals, and though we often volunteered to help, she always wanted to do most of the work. She wasn't much older than all of us but she pretty much treated all of us as her children or siblings.

One distinctive trait about her personality was her serenity. This woman had such an aura of peace around her that we would immediately feel a sense of relief as soon as we walked in that small apartment. In her quiet demeanor, Josée single-handedly silenced the emotional chaos that I would come with to their house from spending a whole week alone in my apartment.

While Josée was the calm to our storms, Félin on the other hand was the captain who taught us how to navigate them. A journalist by profession and a pastor by calling, he's one of those people who maintain their humor in any situation, pleasant or unpleasant. What I remember most about him was his capacity to make us laugh at any time of the day and in any situation, then turn around and lead us to a God-given vision.

Félin is also a man of prayer, and he consistently made sure that we made prayer the first priority of our day. For as long as I can remember, we had a family prayer meeting every morning at 5:00 a.m. This was not dependent on whether we went to bed early or not, whether we were at our own apartments or not. This was dependent on us simply being alive. As long as we were alive and living in the UK, rest assured that Félin would call at 4:50 a.m. to wake us up to pray and give us a portion of Scripture to meditate on. Then, he would call us again at 6.00 a.m. to hear our understanding of that word. This man was relentless! Nevertheless, I will forever be grateful for those early morning prayers. That lifestyle that was instilled in us, got us so disciplined and so focused on our walk with God, and this kept us safe and grounded.

During the week, both Félin and Josée made it a point to call me, check on my day and remind me that I was expected at home on Friday. This family turned my life around, made me enjoy each single day of my life, gave me a sense of belonging, and gave me the emotional security that I had sought for in my first years in London.

Ever since then, they also made it a point to always visit my family in Rwanda whenever they travelled there. My father and mother grew so fond of them and to this day, they always check on us.

Learning to be a girl

If I was to tell you that I grew up a tomboy, would you believe it? Yes, I was for a big part of my life, up until I met Hope Isanga. Hope was one of the teenagers of the Isanga family who attended Zion Temple London. She and her siblings were members of the church choir, Asaph. We were all part of the church youth group and it is from there that we had instantly connected.

One thing that I always loved about Hope was her big heart and even more, her sense of style and fashion. She would come to church with everything about her touched to the detail. I mean, she made me look like I never used the mirror before leaving the house, yet I did.

While I didn't do more than simply comb my hair, spray some perfume, and wear a top and a skirt, Hope could have easily passed for a makeup artist. Her face always looked like those of the celebrities on the cover of an Essence or Ebony magazine. When she came to church, all we would want to do is take a closer look at her. She was that good.

I loved makeup but had no clue on how to apply it. I had grown up seeing my mother make her face up and make sure that she never left the house looking simple. HA! Mom was sophisticated like that. I loved makeup but it seemed too tiresome to apply, even more so after seeing Hope do the extra with eyeshadows, mascara and eyeliners. I mean, I would never attempt to learn that skill, until one day when we had a church wedding to attend and we all had to look our best.

I remember going to Hope's house after her insistent begging to work on my face befitting that wedding ceremony. Let me just say that by the time that she was done working on my face and handed me the mirror, I was smitten by the face that looked back at me. I immediately fell in love with the version of me that looked more of a girl, more ladylike and more polished. From then on, I loved makeup. Even today, when people ask me what one of my favorite things is, I don't hesitate to tell them that it is makeup.

Hope Isanga, the sister that taught me how to always look "sharp".

Another important thing that makeup did for me was to connect a nostalgic part of my heart to my mother sitting in front of her dressing mirror, slowly yet skillfully drawing her eyebrows, lining her lips and adding a touch of lip color to accentuate them. Hope connected me to my mother without knowing it, and till this day, each morning as I get ready for work, I sit and stroke my face with different brushes, add color to my lips, look at myself in the mirror and smile back. It's a ritual of Laurette that I still practice each morning.

Meet my Burundian Sister

I can never reflect on my time in London without thinking of Belyse Kwizera. I simply can't. I met Belyse through the church but also, her family was close friends to Félin Gakwaya's family. We met at least twice a week in our prayer meetings but often, I would visit the Budigoma Family, where she lived. Belyse was and still is the wife of Claude Budigoma, one of the Budigoma brothers and she had recently migrated to London. Belyse was a few years older than me and had recently gotten married and was expecting her first born daughter, Cassey.

We instantly connected and she treated me like her younger sister. I was actually more or less the same age as her younger sister. Very Burundian and, over here, I was very Rwandan but our sisterhood reflected a lot of our similarities as people from those two countries.

I vividly remember our emotional escapes on Wednesday evenings when we would catch the latest episode of DESPERATE HOUSEWIVES and then call each other after to literally gossip about those women on Wisteria Lane. Those evenings helped drown our nostalgia for our relatives back home but also served to start conversations that sisters have about relationships, body image, mental wellbeing and survival.

Belyse was an awesome cook! This woman has magical hands when it comes to cooking! Her baking was amazing. She watched Cooking shows and translated them for me in simple ways in Kirundi that made me learn new dishes. Belyse taught me how to cook "Ikizungu", or say, cook western dishes.

She was that person that I could call and we carry on from where we left off. Those years of our friendship in London gave me a safe space to simply be me, no church duties, no religious lingo, nothing. Me, a teenager, searching for the true meaning of my life and navigating life itself, alone but again, not alone.

Matters of the heart

As humans, we were created for relationships and for love. From when we are born, we all long to be loved and to love, and as we grow, that longing takes different forms. One of those forms is romance. As a person, I am not any different from any other person who first experienced romance in their teens, and that part of my life taught me so much about who I am as a person.

Before I ever fell in love, I didn't know that I was the giddy and over the moon kind of girl. I didn't even recognize that I longed for an emotional connection and companionship, until I met him; A perfect gentleman, kind, well-mannered, and whose presence in my life removed a loneliness I didn't know was there all along.

I met him through a connection of sorts and we had history and so much more in common. He was friendly and his humor made our relationship blossom. He was a great friend, who I could talk to for hours and hours on the phone without getting bored and without being sexual either. I never really felt the need to pretend and be someone else around him, because he accepted me for who I was and what I stood for. I loved being affirmed by him, and his encouragement meant translated into support. With him, I knew that there was nothing I would go through alone. Our relationship felt like drinking a cup of hot chocolate while indoors, on a chilly London rainy day.

It's interesting how, despite the full presence of God in our lives, we still long for such companionship but I discovered that God wired us that way too, to experience humanity and a different kind of love. I was going through so much hardship when he and I met, and at times all I needed was someone to call me and lovingly say, "Mamy wanjye, humura (Hang in there Mama)." I didn't know why then, but those words were so soothing and worked magic on me. Later in life when I came across the bestseller, "THE FIVE LOVE LANGUAGES" by Dr. Gary Chapman, I finally learned that my primary and secondary love languages were Touch and Words of Affirmation and as such, he spoke my language effortlessly. His past experiences and his survival in all of them created so much respect in me for who he was as a person. He loved that I was patriotic and his life taught me so much about love for the nation and love for our people Abanyarwanda. Being raised by a tribe of strong women, he had great skills in communicating to me as a lady and treating me right. Respect for women was and still is paramount for him. Dear reader, like I said, that relationship simply felt like drinking a warm drink in the cold and rainy London weather.

My companionship with him taught me that I am the type who is all in or all out when it comes to relationships. I am the type who loves hard and gives my very best. That relationship matured me and taught me what it really meant to "give" the very best of self, in life.

He taught me how I deserved to be treated, what being cherished looked like and those memories I will forever hold dear. Mind you, we were all believers and sex wasn't on the table; he loved me to later access. It was friendship and love in one. No other conditions. Just that. One evening, while visiting him, I will never forget this, he got a basin, a towel and warm water, sat me down and poured the water on my feet and washed my feet. Goodness! As he washed my feet, his humility and simplicity struck me, there was nothing as powerful and as yielding as that act. He washed my feet and promised to love me, respect me and take care of me for the rest of our lives. This served to build trust in him and commitment.

Yes, I am a hopeless romantic but you, dear reader, should have heard the words that he told me and experienced that moment to roll your eyes as you read this. Hahaha!

He allowed me to experience love in its purest form and for that, I will forever thank God for him and for that season of my life. Oh, young and sweet love!

Surviving the loneliness and strangeness of a foreign land required much more than my personal resilience. It required Friendship. Love. Adoption. Fellowship. The combination of these formed me to become empathetic to people suffering in different emotional ways. I always felt and still do feel that if someone could love me much without knowing me and choosing to welcome me in their life, then I owe it to others to be the same.

If we so long to be loved, accepted and cared for, the least we could do is do the same for others in need of the very same treatment.

Independence taught me the importance of having values as strong anchors of your soul. For then, do we keep our lives grounded.

In the absence of values, there is no telling what we humans are capable of. That season taught me so much about resilience and longsuffering but also the importance of choosing the right people to surround yourself with.

As I reflect on that chapter of my life, I realize that, I couldn't have been who I am today, had I not spent time alone with myself. I couldn't have survived rejection later in life, had I not developed self-reliance from that season.

Indeed, nothing could be more fitting to describe the character forging from that season as the Bible verse, Romans 8:28 (NKJV) puts it; "And we know that all things work together for good to those who love God, to those who are the called according to His purpose.

Chapter Five

Shaped By Volunteering

With friends who were like family around me, I was well settled in my new life. Despite it all though, I couldn't ignore the fact that I missed Rwanda and I missed my family terribly. I missed my church. I missed singing Kinyarwanda hymns. And oh, how I missed listening to sermons by Apostle Paul Gitwaza.
In those days, I would have my mother send me audio tapes and CDs of Christian music and his sermons, and there was nothing I could trade them for. They kept me connected to my homeland. Also, I kept in touch with my church friends from back home, and through them, I was always informed on what was happening in Zion Temple.

Zion Temple London

One day, on a phone call with one of my childhood friends, Natacha Umutoni, I was surprised to learn that Zion Temple would soon be launched in the UK. It had been announced in church that there was going to be a conference to launch it. At the church reception desk, Natacha had managed to get the contacts of the organizers of the launch in London, and she shared them with me. The excitement that I had when she shared those cell phone numbers was immeasurable. As soon as I hung up the phone, I called one of them and was answered by a man called Henry Iradukunda. He gave me the information on the conference and directions to the venue and told me, "See you soon!"

I attended that two-day conference, on a Saturday and Sunday. The main speakers were Apostle Dr. Paul Gitwaza, and an elderly lady fondly known as Mama Domitille. I was well aware of who she was. She had been in Rwanda for the 2002 Africa Arise and Shine (Afrika Haguruka) conference to testify on how she had died and then rose from the dead with a message to evangelize to those who were yet to know the Lord, forewarning them of what was awaiting humanity on the side of eternity. Inviting her to speak to the thirsty and hungry souls in London was the Lord's great plan to start a new wave of revival in the Rwandan and Burundian communities.

On the day I stepped in that small hall in Old Brompton and connected to the Spirit in that room, I knew instantly that my life was about to take another turn. I just knew it deep in my heart.

Throughout the conference, I kept telling my heart, "Barbara, you have so many financial demands on your little funds. You can't commit to travelling to this church every weekend. You just came for the conference, not to rejoin. It will be too much to handle," and the more I tried to convince my soul of this, the more I became convinced that this wouldn't be the end of it.

The conference ended after about three hours and I quickly rushed home without greeting anyone. Old Brompton was far from where I lived and I didn't want to miss my bus home from Heathrow Airport where the underground train route of the Piccadilly Line ended. On the entire way back, given the thoughts that I had kept silencing throughout the conference, I kept thinking to myself, "What does the Holy Spirit want from me?"

Home away from Home

In the following months, I went back to my regular life in Hayes. However, at the back of my mind, I always knew that there was a force calling the deepest parts of my soul to connect with that newly birthed church. I kept feeling a longing and emptiness that I felt could only be filled if I could visit Zion Temple regularly. So, I finally decided to start visiting the church twice a month, and every evening that I did, I had a sense of satisfaction as I headed back home.

A few weeks later, I knew what I had to do, and it was going to be costly. Nonetheless, I knew that I had to move churches and shift permanently to Zion Temple.

The church was in Woodgreen, literally on the end of the underground train route of the Piccadilly line, and I was commuting from the other end near Heathrow Airport. It took me at least two hours to get there, and each trip cost me at least seven pounds. But, I knew that I had to make that decision.

Once I made my decision, I approached my leaders from Assemblée de Dieu and told them that I was making the move but would be visiting back when time permitted. I then moved back home.

Zion Temple was home away from home. This fellowship gave us space to talk, sing and pray in our mother tongue. This church not only gave us a family, but relationships that were so meaningful, especially to those of us who lived away from our families back home. For the first two or three Sundays that I fellowshipped in Zion Temple, I literally felt like a goldfish back in the rich ocean full of those of my kind. Even before meeting Félin and Josée Gakwaya, I would look forward to going to church so much that the two-hour commute meant nothing. Huddled in one of the seats on the train with a book in my hands, I would happily rejoice to go to the house of the Lord.

At the Wood Green underground station, waiting for the Piccadilly line to take me home (Winter 2004).

You can do it

Anyone who knows me will tell you this one thing about me; "Barbara is not one who sits and overlooks while things are not going on well. Barbara is proactive, unless she doesn't know what is needed." I was raised to be responsible and find space to fit in, or create space to operate in. This being said, you will understand how I got involved in ministry and became the person that I am today.

I have always loved helping where need be. When I started attending Zion Temple, I knew that I had to give back and do something in the church. One thing for sure is that joining the choir was out of the question. I mean, people join a church and join the choir, but I knew that despite my love for music, I was far from singing. When it comes to singing amongst other skills, I am honest with myself. I can't sing. I wasn't going to usher people to their seats either, since there were enough beautiful and smartly dressed ladies that were doing an excellent job than I could. So, I sat in the pews and wondered what I could do.

One Sunday, I attended church, and surprisingly, on his way to Brussels where we had another church branch, Apostle Dr. Paul Gitwaza had visited Zion Temple in London for the weekend. We had service like we did ordinarily, but I sat in anticipation, waiting for him to go to the pulpit. Time came and he was welcomed to share the sermon that he had prepared. Alongside him, another gentleman, Celestin Rusengatabaro was invited to interpret for him.

Now, back in 2002, during the Africa Arise conference, I had volunteered to interpret during the conference but I was such a novice then and didn't think that much would come from that episode. So, in the pews in Zion Temple London, on this particular Sunday, I watched Celestin closely and compared him with the different interpreters that I had seen grace the Zion Temple Kigali pulpit. Celestin gave it his very best. He was bold and had a smile on his face as he interpreted the preaching machine that was Paul Gitwaza.

While following the sermon and also watching Celestin, I heard a voice tell me, "Barbara, you know you can volunteer and give interpretation a try! You might actually find that you can do it faster," and just like that, that soul conversation I tended to have with this smooth yet convincing voice that got me here in the first place started again.

I resolved that I was not going to be a pushover. I mean, I was a newcomer and these people didn't really know me, plus I didn't think that I could do it. So, I told that voice, "If the occasion ever arises, I will offer to volunteer. But in the meantime, let me just sit and soak all of this in."

Stepping Up

The occasion eventually came during a conference for the commemoration of the Genocide against the Tutsi in London. This two-day healing conference took place during the commemoration weekend of April 2004, and we had many speakers and guests who would need interpretation.

I attended the conference not planning to do anything, but for some reason, as I was getting ready at home to attend the conference, the smooth voice told me, "Barbara, dress up. You have a lot of work to do today." I obeyed and dressed up well in a grey pleated skirt and a nice warm top with some boots. It was in the winter and I commuted a long distance, so I needed to be well covered.

Since I had trained myself to be led by that voice and had never been disappointed, I had a feeling that this conference would be full of surprises. Indeed, there were surprises.

It turns out that on that particular Saturday, Celestin wasn't feeling well and someone was needed to fill in for him for the whole conference. Guess who volunteered! I did. I was seated in my chair, waiting for the conference to start when I overheard the church leaders saying that Celestin was sick and not coming to the conference.

As soon as I heard them share their concerns on who was going to step in, the smooth voice came to me and whispered, "Barbara, this is the occasion that you asked for. Stand and go volunteer in the place of Celestin."

I mustered all the courage I could, knowing that this was going to be my first time to stand in front of many people. I knew that I just had to do it, so I approached the organizing team. I greeted them and told them, "My name is Barbara. I overhead you saying that you needed an interpreter. I don't have a lot of experience, but I have done this in Zion Temple Kigali. Maybe I can try to help today."

Although all I had done was sit next to guests and whisper in their ears and hope for the best, but saying, "I have done this in Kigali" made it seem like I was a pro. I had to at least build some sense of confidence that I could at least try. I was going to stand in front of hundreds this time, and I had to be bold enough to dare to do it.

The leading team members that I talked to were Félin Gakwaya and Richard Budigoma. The two men looked at me and then looked at each other and smiled. They didn't really know me then, but they needed help. So, they looked at me and said, "Let's talk to Pastor Dieudonné Vuningoma and get back to you."

Pastor Dieudonné Vuningoma was the visiting pastor from Kigali, and he too didn't know me. As they discussed amongst themselves, more guests walked in and the conference would start soon.

Finally, Pastor Dieudonné came to me and told me, "Alright. I don't really know you, but you can try today and we will see how it goes." Like I said, I had never been on the pulpit. But, there was no other way of knowing if I could really pull it off besides letting me try.

The conference opened with singing from the Asaph London choir, and in my seat, my nerves were on edge. In my mind, I kept thinking, "Why did I seriously offer to volunteer? Couldn't I just sit and leave it alone?" until I was called to the stage with Pastor Dieudonné, Praying, trembling, scared, frozen and unsure of myself, I took the microphone, looked at the audience, slowly took it all in and stepped into my moment. The rest is history.

Interpreting for the first time at the pulpit, in the healing conference organized by Zion Temple at the occasion of commemorating the Genocide against the Tutsi. Here, I stood next to Brother Richard Budigoma, one of the church elders at the time

Showing up with all of me

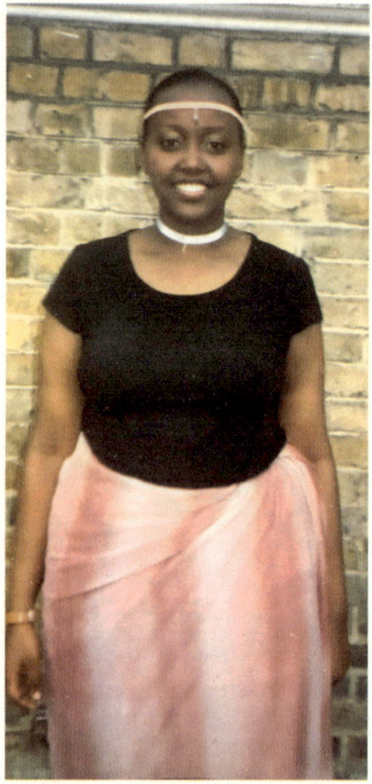

Standing outside the church building after dancing to catch a breath of fresh air before changing again to interpret the sermon.

In Zion Temple London, I found myself so comfortable doing two things; dancing our traditional dance, and interpreting. I loved dancing because it connected me to a piece of my mother, and I loved interpreting because I felt lighter holding the microphone.

The church had room for anyone willing to volunteer, in whatever capacity that they were able to contribute. On special occasions when we had to dance, I would gladly do both. I would dance, then quickly change back to my smart clothes and get ready for the sermon. I worked often as an interpreter for the preachers, and a colleague would work with the moderator of the service.

In the process, my passion for the knowledge of the scriptures grew. Coupled with my love for reading, I would say that this was a time that God prepared me for the work that He was calling me to do. At the time, I honestly didn't think so. I just felt that I was giving this task my best and showing up fully. That's all that mattered... Showing up and giving God the best in that moment.

A helping hand and a need

My committed involvement in the church, despite my young age, caught the attention of my leaders...Bishop Laurent Mukwiza in particular. Bishop Mukwiza had come to the UK to serve as a missionary to Zion Temple London.

We connected instantly and he committed to mentoring me and giving me Bible Studies. There was time for Bible studies for the whole church, but whenever I could make it to the meeting venue before everyone else, we would have a head start. He would give me assignments and I would bring them to him for review.

Bishop Mukwiza was such a father figure in my life. His own first born, Nshuti Trésor, was the same age as I, and that gave me and the Bishop such a bond. Bishop Mukwiza literally treated me like his own daughter to the point that he would regularly check on me and my academic performance. Alongside Félin, Bishop Mukwiza held my hand in those years. In the difficult times of my life, he stood with and prayed for me. Today, when we meet, he still treats me like his adoptive daughter.

Over the time that I was in London, I learned so much from him as his interpreter. He was more of a teacher and he gave me time to catch up. Serving alongside him was so comfortable. I had adjusted to his pace and became so confident that I could interpret for any preacher…or so I thought!

After the Sunday evening service, I always took time to pray with Bishop Mukwiza Laurent

Standing next to a giant

At a conference that Zion Temple London organized, Apostle Gitwaza was invited as the main speaker. Bishop Mukwiza sat me down a few days to the conference and told me that there was a need for someone to interpret for the Apostle and he believed that I was the best fit. I didn't believe the same. I mean, this was Apostle Gitwaza, one of the famous preachers in Kigali. Where was I going to get the speed to interpret for him? First of all, I didn't think I was mature or spiritual enough to stand next to him, and I also didn't think that I was anointed or even holy enough. Ok, none of this meant anything. I was simply afraid. This was way above my league, but by the looks of things, I was still going to serve alongside the Apostle.

Bishop Mukwiza must have seen that I was nervous and ready to chicken out, and he informed Apostle Gitwaza that he was proposing I work with him. He assured him that I had worked with him for a while and I was good. He basically saw the need and the opportunity to put me on the next level, and I will forever be grateful to him for the trust he put in me.

The Saturday afternoon came and the conference was in Oxford. The conference had attracted around three hundred people, excluding the children. That was a huge number in Europe and in the Rwandan-Burundian community. To say that I was nervous would be an understatement. I just felt like running away. I looked at how exposed I would be, the people that would spend hours looking at me and wondering why it was me standing up there, and above all that, I was afraid of disappointing God and myself. Then there was the fear that I had of fainting in front of that whole congregation. I seriously believed that I could faint in front of that congregaton. I had terrible stage fright.

Also, back in the day, Apostle Gitwaza was one of those preachers that you either connected and worked well with from the beginning, or he sat you down because you didn't meet his expectations. So, you understand why I was too nervous. I could picture him turning to his left and looking at me and saying, "God bless you, young lady, but I don't think this is working well. Please go back to your seat. Congregation, please give her a round of applause for doing a great job. God bless you." Ha!

The moderation of the conference went too fast, and he was soon called to the stage. I shyly walked up there, took the microphone in my hand and prayed in my heart, "God, you started this. I didn't reach here by myself. Please use me and kindly save me the embarrassment of fainting or not doing this well and being benched."

The first few minutes were easy because he spent his time connecting to the audience, passing regards, cracking a few jokes, and he spoke slowly. I managed well. Then, he entered into the sermon, read the verses and ran with them until the end. I got out of my head and decided to picture myself alone in that hall with him, and God sitting in the sanctuary. I set it in my mind that I was going to interpret for God alone. I set in my mind the momentary assumption that God didn't speak Kinyarwanda, and I was going to give it my best to deliver this sermon to Him in the best English that I knew. That was it.

We had spoken for about three hours when he closed, and to both our surprise, we had maintained a connection yet it was my first time. Alas! I wasn't benched. I had gotten my formula for not failing...Keeping God as the focus of what I did. That was the first time I ever stood next to the Apostle, and that day chartered an inconceivable path to what God had in store for me.

Giving my time, with a committed heart to a cause that I didn't calculate any material gain was the most satisfying endeavor that I ever engaged in. It has often been said that to give is better than to receive. I am a witness of that. Offering myself as a living sacrifice, as the Bible calls it, is the best way to approach volunteering. When you offer yourself, you are not calculating what is in it for you. You are not looking at the gains and, in my case, I did this for God and for His church. Nonetheless, at the core of it all, I gave myself for the betterment of people and I have been graciously rewarded.

This season taught me one great value; SACRIFICE. In one or more ways than one, whether we know it or not, SACRIFICE is rewarded. SACRIFICE teaches you, it shapes you and most definitely, it equips you. From these experiences, I made up my mind that whenever I engage in any activity, first and foremost, I will seek the betterment of people who will benefit from my engagement. In the process, I became and I evolve to become a better person.

In the early days (Summer 2005) when I had just started interpreting for Apostle at our local Zion Temple church in Wood Green. In the picture, Apostle Dr. Paul Gitwaza was giving an example with the help of Emmanuel Mpendo, one of our choir singers.

Chapter Six

Shaped By Dilemma

When I went to the UK, I got into the immigration system as a minor seeking asylum. As the system permitted, those seeking asylum were granted either definite or indefinite leave to remain in the UK, which simply meant that some got permanent residence and others didn't. For those who didn't, they were given some years or months in most cases, after which they could apply for an extension or permanent residence. As for me, I didn't get the permanent residence, but I kept hoping that I would get it when my time to apply for an extension came. The process of applying for an extension was quite tedious. It meant that I had to reconnect with my lawyer, revisit my case, reapply and wait. The waiting had such an emotional toll on me. I did not have the assurance for my future and I did not know if I would ever get stable. I could only hope that my application wouldn't end with a denial. I basically hung in limbo and hoped for the best for a period of two years.

A consistent voice and a frightening message

Eighteen years old, independent, living alone, stable and ready to apply for my permanent residence, I was excited for a better future that I knew awaited me. I had finally found my footing in this new life. I had friends, I had family and I was doing so well academically. I had begun to love my stay in the UK when my time to reapply for permanent residence came.

I took time to pray for God's favor and the grace to finally get my permanent residence. I was very hopeful and I knew that God had my life in His hands. His faithfulness in the two years' prior had shown me that He had great plans for my life and I simply needed to trust Him and let Him lead. Indeed, God had great plans for my life, but they were not what I envisioned. What I felt in my spirit during those days of prayer could have never crossed my mind.

One evening, when I was breaking my fast, I heard the Spirit whisper to me, "Barbara, I have great plans for your life, but they do not involve staying in the UK!" The initial shock and fear that I had when I heard those words took me aback. "What? No!" God couldn't just show up and tell me that the now enjoyable chapter of my life was coming to an end. "No!" It felt unfair. Uprooting my life again was frightening. So, how did

I react to that voice? I silenced it. I ignored it. I fought it and I completely refused to process the message it had given me.

I stayed on course with my initial plans, and applied for my permanent residence and went on to live like nothing happened. The process took a whole year. In June 2005, I was denied permanent residence, but I persisted with legal support. At the same time, I tried to convince God with desperate prayers; "God, I will do anything for you. I will give you anything that you want, but please help me stay here. I need to stay here. I need to get my education. I need to do something substantial with my life. Please, I beg you…just this once. Make this work out for me…just this once. I promise I will never ask for anything else!" Oh, how short sightedness hindered me from really seeing God's big dream for my life!

Well, suffice to say that, that prayer was answered with a stronger voice and a stronger message: "Barbara, your life here has come to an end. I want you to cancel your application, tell the truth and get ready to move back to Rwanda. Your life will begin in Rwanda. You are needed back home. From there, I will bless you. I will bless the work of your hands. I will lift you beyond your years. I will give you a name. I will sit you in high places that you never imagined possible, and I will build your life. My dream for your life will begin in Rwanda!"

More clear, concise and directional, this message simply shook me and in my mind, I kept thinking, "How are you going to go back to Rwanda without a degree?

What work will you do? What will you tell your parents? What life will you live?" My future was blurred and according to my human understanding, very bleak. So, scared and unsure of what the future held for me, I rebelled and persisted with my application.

At this point, I stopped praying about it because, obviously, God had made Himself clear on where He wanted me, and I wasn't going to listen to Him. Instead, I took my own route and disobeyed Him, which gave me a sense of control, and also that of fear of an impending doom. At the back of my mind, I knew this God too well. As always, He would easily find a way to get His way, even though I wasn't going down without a fight. How foolish I was! Jonah should have been my role model.

As you would expect, all my applications were denied. And on top of that, a new law was passed, that for asylum seekers whose cases were denied multiple times, there would be no legal aid available for them. This meant that legal fees would no longer be covered for me, which of course had a negative impact on me. My lawyer dropped my case and gave me the alternative of seeking legal aid from a non-profit volunteer firm that was based in Central London, to see if they could at least go with me to court for assistance. He was gracious enough to inform me that that legal firm was overwhelmed by the overload of cases dropped in that season, and told me not to get my hopes up but start preparing myself to appear in court alone.

All the while, in my spirit, I knew what I had to do but was too afraid to do it. I kept insisting, but for some reason also, I had peace in knowing the outcome of my desperate efforts. I knew that I was going to keep getting denials until I surrendered to God, but I also wanted to keep trying, hoping that He would see my efforts and just give in. As if God can be manipulated! Ha! He must have laughed at my attempts to get Him to change His mind.

My unbelievable future

As I chased a permanent residence, I spent a lot of time in prayer and supplication. I was either praying to God to cave in just this once, or interceding for my future, which was quite uncertain for me in those days. I reasoned; if I was to return to Rwanda, I would be reunited with my family, which was a great thing, but building life again from scratch right after doing the same in a foreign country would be too much to handle. So, I kept praying and asking God for His grace.

Over the next few months, I started having different visions about my life. They were surreal and would come to me at different times of the day or the night. Two of those visions were distinct. In one, I saw myself standing in front of thousands of people in a stadium, preaching. In the other one,

I saw myself in my mother church in Kigali, standing next to Apostle Paul Gitwaza and speaking alongside him.

These visions didn't really make sense but they were too real, and I knew that they meant to show me where my future was heading. I couldn't believe what I saw. It seemed too grandiose for me, and it also wasn't anything that had ever crossed my mind. Public speaking was nothing I had aspired or hoped to do.

The visions evolved to an audible voice that constantly told me, "Barbara, your blessing is not in this country. Your blessing is in Rwanda. The sooner you accept that, the sooner and closer you will get to your blessing." With time, I began to accept the possibility of daring to take God's vision for my life as the direction that was the best fit for me. As acceptance settled in, fear melted away and I stopped trying to convince God to see things my way. Instead, I prepared myself to walk in His way, and in doing so, I stepped into my destiny with Him.

As my court date approached, I went to Central London to look for pro bono solicitors in that recommended firm who could assist me with my court hearing. I got an appointment after waiting in a queue for more than four hours alongside other asylum seekers who were in desperate conditions like I was. After getting my appointment, I met the lady who was assigned to meet us. She requested for my file, which I gave her after explaining to her my predicament. The next day, I showed up at the firm office at 6:00a.m., only to land in another long line of about seventy people.

Eventually, my turn came and I was shown to a small cubicle. I took a seat and the lady who had stayed with my file sat opposite me and opened my case file. She told me, "Barbara, thank you for considering us to be of assistance to you at this time. I have looked at your file with my colleagues, and unfortunately, we can't represent you. You will have to appear in court alone and represent yourself. Thank you for your understanding."

I was not surprised. I knew that nothing was going to come out of that encounter. I was just going through the formalities. The whole while, that voice was saying, "Barbara, this will give you the space to express yourself and share your truth. I am with you." I returned home and mentally prepared myself for my court hearing. I had never heard of anyone doing what I was about to do. It was going to be a major showdown, and I seriously didn't know how to go about it.

I shared my predicament with my senior pastor, Bishop Mukwiza Laurent, and my dear friend and brother, Pastor Félin Gakwaya. As expected, they didn't want to influence me in any way, so they both offered to pray for me to be attentive and really follow God's will for my life. They encouraged me to be open and to let God take the lead, and so I did. In hindsight, they were well aware of the implications of such a decision and they wanted me to be sure that it was indeed from a divine guidance. I remember having many sessions with them to process this and I remember them telling me to be absolutely sure that it was God. I could tell that it was heavy for them too, I mean, they were going to be blamed as my guardians for having allowed me to choose such a path despite the opportunities that I had ahead of me. When I left the UK, so many people in our community blamed them for "encouraging" me and others simply decided that they had brainwashed me into doing this. Which wasn't the case at all. It wasn't easy for them too because, on the other side of the coin, they didn't want me to miss God's plan for my life, even as frightening as it was. It was a dilemma for all of us.

The D Day

My court date finally arrived. I got myself ready, dressed smartly and headed to the Hatton Cross Tribunal Hearing Centre. My hearing was at 2:00 p.m. I arrived early and just sat and waited. I was not worried or afraid. I had already made peace with where God was going to take my life, and I was just going through the necessary procedure.

While I was waiting, I saw Chantal "Bobette" Gakwaya, Pastor Félin's sister, walk in the waiting area. She looked at me and told me, "We can't let you go through this alone. I came to stand with you and pray for you. Do not worry. It will all go well."

At 2:00 p.m., I was called to the courtroom, shown my seat and informed that I would stand when the judge walked in. Shortly after, the judge walked in and we all stood. As he sat down, we were also allowed to sit down. He introduced himself and asked the Home Office solicitor to present himself. Thereafter, the Home Office solicitor led the discussion and informed us all of the situation of my case.

He then stood up and presented to the judge a copy of the expert report on Rwanda; on which his arguments were going to based. He also handed me one and said, "Ms. Barbara, we do hope that your account will correlate to what is written in the expert report on Rwanda."

At that moment, I felt like God had made sure that I wouldn't back down. The only way was through that process, and even if I tried to circumvent it, that expert report would pin me down and I would lose my case miserably.

Once the Home Office solicitor had presented his arguments, he gave me the platform to express myself. I took a deep breath, said a short prayer and let myself go. I felt a wave of strength engulf me and I opened my mouth and presented my argument. I thanked the judge and the Home Office solicitor for the opportunity to share my story, and then said, "I am recanting on the facts stated in my claim for asylum. I am not a refugee and I believe that as a Christian, I need to tell the truth. I came to the UK to look for better opportunities, to acquire a great education and to be able to do something with my life, but the means that I used were wrong, and for that I apologize. I believe that God wants me to return to my mother country and if need be, maybe one day He will bring me back to this country to be a blessing." And with those words, I was relieved. I felt like a tone of weight had been lifted off my shoulders. I breathed lightly and I knew instantly that I was going to be on a wild ride with God.

Both the judge and the solicitor never saw that coming. They turned red and were at a loss for words. The judge looked at me and asked, "Young woman, are you sure and conscious of what you have just done?" to which I responded, "Yes, your honor." The solicitor proceeded to say, "Your honor, I do not think there is anything more that we can say at this time, but to close her case."

The judge, in shock, stared at me and said, "Ms. Barbara, in my entire career, I have never met anyone as bold and courageous as you. At your age, looking at what you have just lost, to stand and speak the truth, I simply find that commendable and honorable. If it was up to me, I would grant you citizenship if I wasn't bound by the law. I will ask the Home Office however, to grant you time to finish your studies and prepare yourself to return home. And when ready, just contact your social worker to arrange for your return." The solicitor agreed to advocate for that request at the Home Office, given that the circumstances were special, and would be getting back to me on the final decision.

And just like that, my case was closed on that day.

Shocking revelation

Now that it was clear and settled that I would be returning to Rwanda, there was one more thing left to do. For so long, I had lived with the secret that was that decision, and kept it from my parents. I knew that they had a different world perspective from mine, and I understood and respected that. But, I also recognized that I had grown and was in a position to make my own decisions, and of course be ready for the consequences that would spring from those decisions. I was ready to assume the responsibilities that came with the decision to return to Rwanda with no college degree and meaningful professional work experience, but I was afraid for my parents and their dreams for me that I had just shattered.

I prayed day and night for an opportunity to face my father and tell him that I was returning to Rwanda soon, and not as the medical doctor that he had sent me to become. It was fitting that we have this conversation in person, not on the phone, and God granted me that request.

In July 2006, Papa came to London to visit, on his way to Belgium to visit my mother who had gone there for medical treatment. He spent three weeks in London and it was so refreshing to see him again after so many years. We literally talked through the four years that I had been in London, my life, my education and dreams for the future, minus the pending return to Rwanda that I had not yet mustered the courage to share with him.

One evening, as we were on the train heading to Central London to get his bus to Brussels, I finally broke the news to him. Talk about bad timing! Fidgeting, I looked at him and said, "Papa, I have some big news to share with you. They are not good news, but I have to share this with you. I am coming back to Rwanda for good next year. I cancelled my application for permanent residence."

The shock on his face was undeniable, but what I didn't expect was his laugh and response. "Barbara, ndabizi ko kuva cyera uri umusazi, kandi ukora ibikujemo (Barbara, I know that you've always been crazy, and you do whatever comes to your mind)! This is a great disappointment but you will always be welcome home."

The last visit that Papa made to the UK before I returned home, to Rwanda for good (June 2006)

Papa didn't belittle me. He didn't make me feel like it was the end of the world, but I indeed saw the disappointment in his eyes. I saw the pain of unfulfilled dreams for his daughter, but I also saw relief that I was coming home. What I saw in his eyes gave me the resolve to promise myself that I would do everything in my capacity to make him proud one day. For some reason, I felt like I owed him so much for his shattered dreams.

As soon as Papa reached Brussels and visited Mama in the hospital where she was, he shared the news with her and told her that she would be seeing me sooner than expected. She wasn't angry either. Mama had been sick for a while now and wanted to see me, so this came as good news for her.

The rest, we would figure it out as a family.

Life is full of dilemmas. These dilemmas always drive us to make decisions and they test our growth and capacity to stand in the face of storms that come with the decisions that we take. My dilemma took me to a place where I didn't understand and nor could I ask my loved ones to understand or even support me. On that journey of uncertainty, I discovered that God has a knack for meeting people in hard places and transforming lives in the wilderness of life. It is in the wild that He shows Himself strong but also, teaches us key life lessons.

My dilemma taught me deep faith. Faith for the future. Faith for a better unknown. I came to find that in those times, God is greater in the wild than in the domesticated and lavish palaces that we so eagerly ask Him to sit us in. Dilemmas are places of limbo. If one doesn't move on fast and swiftly, they risk stagnating and never fully discovering what God had in store for them all along.

Dear friend reading this book, let me tell you this; in the end, it will all be worthwhile. In the end, it will all make sense.

Chapter Seven

Shaped By Decisions

One of the greatest blessings of my life was living alone in England. I count it a great blessing because it gave way to a relationship with God that I didn't know was possible.

Living with God as a young woman

When I moved to the UK, I found myself out of the crowd, out of peer pressure and alone. I had a lot of time to sit and reflect on who I was as a person, what I battled with in life and what I overcame, what I failed at and what I dreamed of achieving.

I learned the true meaning of being led by the Holy Spirit, engaging and involving Him in every single decision that I made, including what to cook, when to do my laundry, when to relate with my neighbors, and so much more. At the time, being alone just made me more aware of His presence in my life than any other time. I grew deeper in the knowledge of the Word as I spent a lot of time trying to understand Him and involve Him according to His Word in my life. I was privileged to walk such a precious journey with God in my youth and I know that today, I am so much of the person that He formed in those years alone.

You will be surprised at what you can process in the absence of the crowd. There are so many victories that will be won if and only if one retreats to that secret place where they are by themselves. In that zone, one has no choice but to be honest with him/herself and deal with some unresolved issues, and that will help one acquire a new resolve to advance further in life.

In my case, living in London alone gave me that space to discover who I was, to forge the kind of person that I wanted to become, and to set myself on a path towards the kind of life I wanted to live. Today, when I look back, I realize that decisions I made in those five years living in West Drayton shaped the person that I am in more ways than one.

Moving back to Rwanda

The last two weeks of my time in London were the most exciting, and the hardest. I was excited to be going back home, knowing that I had put everything that mattered to me as a young person on hold for God's calling over my life. However, although my heart was sure that all would be well, my mind often played games on me. "Barbara, you have lost your mind! What are you going to do in Rwanda without a degree?" "Barbara, God talks to pastors and you are not one. You made these thoughts up in your mind." "Barbara, what will you tell people? They will think that you are crazy. Are you sure it was God who truly said you should go back? Barbara, does God even talk?" My thoughts were in constant conflict with one other sentence that also ran through my mind; "I will never leave you nor forsake you."

I tried to keep a positive outlook on the whole situation and remind myself that my family was doing well, that I wasn't going to be a burden and that I was still too young and could still pursue an education in Rwanda and make something of myself, besides, the West wasn't paradise and I could simply start afresh and succeed. God didn't bless the West alone and write off the rest of the world, so it wasn't all bad.

The other hard thing I went through in those two weeks was calling friends and family to tell them of the decision that I had made, and how I was returning home for good. All were shocked and angry that I could do something as crazy as that. Some were not kind, some flat out insulted me, but I was fine with it. I had learned a long time ago that in life, not everyone will see things the same way you do, but that shouldn't deter you from living out your convictions.

From left to right, my brothers; Patrick Mpfizi and Aggrey Mpfizi

I had made the decision to never be a people-pleaser from the moment that I started living alone, and I wasn't about to start then or apologize for making "crazy" decisions. So, what did I do? I thanked them for their concerns and just focused on the new chapter of my life that was about to unfold.

Even though I lost friends, I offered myself the gift of living in authenticity.

Reconnections - A blessing in disguise

I arrived in Kigali on an Ethiopian flight on Saturday, July 7th 2007 in the afternoon. The moment I stepped off the plane, I felt warm. I felt alive. I felt like I was at the right place and at the right time. This didn't just feel like returning home after so many years of being homesick. This simply felt right.

Being away from home had left a gap in my relationship with my brothers, and coming back gave me new opportunities to reconnect with them and get to learn more about them. They had grown and changed, and I was also a different person. We had so much catching up to do.

Returning home also allowed me to reconnect with my friends from back in the day. I was surrounded by people who knew me, who wanted to know the new me, and people I wanted to make new memories with. I was in for great life experiences.

Doubt is never far

AAs I settled into my new life and new routines, I didn't have a lot to do besides staying at home with Mama or going to church to attend the Africa Haguruka conference that had just started on the weekend I flew back home.

That first week was extraordinary. My spirit was filled with so much nourishment that I could feel a difference in my life compared to when I was away. When the conference ended, I stayed at home with my mother and simply paid attention to the new dynamics of our family.

Within a couple of months, I eventually began to wonder, "How am I going to get a job without any substantive academic achievement?" "What work am I going to do without any relevant professional experience?"

I simply didn't know what was next. Yes, I knew that I would find myself in the church, but I didn't think that it was time for that either.

Doubt had started to kick in. I began to question if I had not rushed to come back. I started thinking that maybe had I waited for a few more years and seen how things turned out, I could have come back in a better position to make a lasting impact for my life, family and community.

One day, Papa sat me down and told me that I needed to go back to school. Since I had studied Psychology and felt like that's what I wanted to keep on studying, I decided to go to the National University of Rwanda in Huye (in the Southern province of Rwanda) to get registered for the new academic year.

I would travel there every early morning to sort out the registration process and return in the evening. It was pretty exhausting but I had to do it. I needed an education and by the look of things, my visions were simply those…visions.

As required at the university, I had to sit for EPLM, a language exam, French to be specific, which I did and returned to Kigali to await my results. In a week, I returned to Huye to check on them and to my surprise, I couldn't find myself on the list. Apparently, some copies had gotten lost, mine included. I was going to have to retake the paper, which I wasn't excited about.

On the drive back to Kigali, I felt uneasy and confused. I prayed and asked God, "Is this really what You want me to do? What happened to what You told me that I was going to do in Rwanda? Should I retake this paper?" Deep in thought, I wondered if I should maybe put my academic pursuits on hold and keep focusing on my mother for a few months while my path becomes clearer. Along the way, I received a phone call that disrupted my thoughts and abruptly reset me back on the divine path that I had begun in London a few years back.

I answered and heard a man say, "Yesu ashimwe (Praise Jesus). Is this Barbara?" to which I responded, "Yes, this is she. Who am I speaking to?" "My name is Jeff and I am Apostle's driver. Mother, Apostle's wife has asked that I call to inform you that we will pick you up this evening as we head to the airport to pick him up. Actually, Apostle specifically requested that you come to the airport with his family to receive him and the guests that he'll arrive with."

One moment, I was so tired from my trip, deep in thought, wondering where my life was going, and the next I was on a call being told that the Apostle had asked that I come to pick him and his guests at the airport? That was strange. There was no familiarity between me and him, or his family for me to pick him at the airport.

I immediately asked Jeff, "So, which apostle are you talking about?" and he laughed and responded, "Apostle Gitwaza." I am sure that Jeff didn't understand my confusion, but his laugh communicated confusion on his part too, since I wasn't a regular in the church circles to be called upon in such a way. We both laughed and then agreed to meet in the area known as Giporoso, which is on the way to Kigali International Airport.

I reached Kigali at around 5:00 p.m. and went straight home to freshen myself up, then walked to Giporoso, which wasn't far from my childhood home, to wait for Jeff and Apostle Gitwaza's family. They pulled over by me at almost 7:00 p.m., and Apostle's wife greeted me and opened the car door for me to enter. In the car were Pastor Consolée Nahoza (Apostle's sister) and some other family members. We shared some small talk before I went quiet all the way to the airport. After the security check at the entrance of the airport, we went to the waiting area and waited for Apostle and his guests.

I was silent the entire time, just wondering why I was there. Being nervous made me think that we waited for what seemed like an eternity, but it was only forty five minutes. The arrival doors suddenly flung open, and Apostle Gitwaza walked through with two American women, one young and another elderly.

Courtney, the Colorado girl

Apostle Gitwaza greeted his wife first and introduced his guests to her and the rest of the party before walking up to me with a beaming smile. He then called the American ladies and looked at me and said, "Barbara, thank you for coming to the airport. God bless you! I want to introduce you to these ladies. This is Courtney Cole and her mother, Catherine.

They are my guests from Colorado. We are now going to my house for dinner. Can you please join us?" to which I responded, "Yes please. I will join you."

I was even more confused, but seeing his American guests made me suspect that I was going to help interpret for them. That made more sense.

With Courtney Cole Ndayishimiye, one morning in the church office.

On our way from the airport, I drove with a family friend and went to Apostle's home. At his house, we found even more of his family, friends and some of his colleagues waiting for him. It was a proper party. Food and soft drinks were served, and people were enjoying the company.

While they all talked amongst themselves, I started talking to Courtney and got to know where she was coming from. I wasn't my usual bubbly self since I was in a new environment that I wasn't accustomed to and Courtney was pretty much quiet and tired from such a long flight from the U.S.A.

Once everyone had finished their meal, Apostle stood to give a speech. He thanked everyone for coming to share dinner with his family. He then introduced Courtney as the young lady that the Lord had assigned to his care. She was coming to stay in Rwanda for a while and she would also be working at the church as his personal Administrative assistant and Catherine, her adoptive mother was here for a short time and would be returning to America.

In my mind, it all made sense. I was here to assist with communication and I didn't mind. After that speech, we had a moment of prayer and then Apostle and his wife escorted us outside the gate.

At the gate, Apostle shook my hand and told me, "Barbara, can you please come back tomorrow at 11:00 a.m.? I want to have a detailed conversation with you."

I accepted that invitation, but at the back of my mind, I somewhat felt that I was going to be requested to assist his guests. Nothing more. Little did I know that what would start out as me interpreting for Courtney and Catherine would actually turn out to be me walking in the door to my destiny.

We bid our farewells and I went back home. I didn't know what to make of that whole encounter but I felt at peace.

Between hard places

As requested by Apostle, the next morning I made my way to his house. I was there on time. I was welcomed and sat in the living room where I waited for him to come and meet me. While I waited, Courtney and Catherine came over and greeted me before going to get ready.

Shortly, Apostle walked into the living room and greeted us. We took a few minutes and prayed for the conversation that we were about to have. We said our "Amens" and he turned to look at me, and smiled.

He said, "Barbara, I believe that God sent you to this country for His work. Are you ready? The time has come. You are in Rwanda for the same reason that Courtney is here; for the both of you to serve Him in this season. You will need to be fully engaged in the ministry and working as staff at the church. She will be my personal administrative assistant and you will work alongside her as the church secretary."

I looked at him in shock at how he could just tell me that and I quickly pointed out, "Apostle, I know that God sent me here to serve Him and to take care of some family matters, but I don't think that I want to work at a church. I am applying to start my university studies in Huye."

Yes, I knew that God had called me to serve back home in Rwanda…but to work at a church, at my age? Fulltime? Nope! That wasn't happening! I was young, yes. I was a Christian, yes. But, I wanted my freedom. I wanted to live my life. I wanted to be young and live out my youth. Plus, I didn't think that I had the emotional energy to combine that job with the toll of taking care of my ailing mother.

Further, I was aware that working at the church full time meant that I wouldn't live a simple and ordinary young person's life. I would be judged even more by my peers, and I didn't want that. Besides, I wanted to finish school, get a job and just occasionally help at the church whenever I could. Working full time at the church meant that I would have to make a major detour in life and put my academic plans on hold…or so I reasoned. Ha! What was a more major detour than leaving my comfortable life in London?

Apostle, not being a pushover, especially when it comes to life choices, looked at me and smiled again, as if he knew so much more than he was letting on, he said, "Can you please take time to pray about it and ask God to show you what you are meant to be doing in this season?" I agreed that I would take time to pray for that decision and get back to him after knowing what I was going to do with my life.

It seemed like a negotiation, but funnily, I had already made the decision to move back for exactly what he was asking me to do. I was just so stubborn and fearfully processing this straightforward request.

Apostle asked me, "In the meantime as you pray," and he smiled again, "can you please help Courtney and Catherine for a few days as they visit the city and as Courtney settles to work at the church? She will need an interpreter, but it won't be permanent. If at some point you feel like you can't do it anymore, we will get someone else to hire to work with her."

That was reasonable. As long as it wasn't a proper job at the church, I could do it. We agreed on this temporary assistance, and that was it. Shortly after that conversation, we took our ride through the city with Jeff, Apostle's driver.

I spent the following week at the church helping Courtney to settle in, and we became friends in the process. I got to learn more about her life back in the U.S, her background and why she dared to make the decision to move to Rwanda on a one way ticket. She didn't know when she would be returning home, and I felt for her. It was so hard. She reminded me of the first years that I settled in London, away from home and my culture. I felt like I owed her kindness in this foreign land just like I had received kindness from strangers back when I lived in London.

In that same week, I took time to pray for the decision to work full time at the church, and with each passing day, I began to feel like I actually enjoyed going to the church every morning. I would be at the office from 9:00 a.m. to 5:00 p.m. on the days that we didn't have the weekly service. On Tuesdays and Thursdays, during the weekly service, I would sit next to Courtney and interpret for her and Catherine.

One evening, after one of the church services, I was filled with a peace about working at the church, and I knew that I was going to take on that job. I had one problem though. I didn't know how I was going to inform my father about that decision. I was putting academic pursuits on hold for a period of time that I didn't know and I knew that wouldn't be good news for him. Understandably so. I had already disappointed him so much with my return and now, this was going to be a major blow to his soul. So, I uttered a short prayer and said, "Father, this is your will but please help my father to accept this decision. This was never his dream for my life but help him understand me at least."

I was nervous as I made my way home. I really felt like I was hurting him too much by not having achieved what he wanted me to achieve, but there was no way around it either.

I reached home to find him sitting in the backyard. He greeted me and asked me to sit next to him, as if he already knew what I was about to tell him, and that was nerve-wracking.

In a sort of thoughtful trance, he looked at me and said, "Barbara, I have been observing you. You go to church every morning and return in the evening. I see that you are enjoying yourself. Since your academic plans seem to be on hold, you will need a job and keep yourself busy. Can you ask Apostle Gitwaza to hire you for whatever it is that you have been doing instead of working for free? The income could help you get through as you plan for the future."

I can't explain both the relief and the shock that this gave me! I sat there struck by how God had seemingly answered my prayer that quickly, but also relieved that my father was the one who started that conversation. I didn't delay or hesitate to tell my father of the proposal that Apostle had given me and how I was still thinking about it. He told me to take the opportunity and see where it would take me. What a relief!

The next morning, I went to church and told Apostle of my conversation with my father and how I was on board working full time for the church. He didn't seem surprised. He didn't say it but his attitude did; "It's about time" was the expression on his face.

The Confirmation

Now that I had finally made my decision and was ready to start walking the path that God had charted for me, all that was left was for Apostle to share his vision. One morning at church, he called Courtney and I for an impromptu meeting in his office.

We went to his office and sat adjacent to each other and him sitting opposite us. He looked at us and said, "I am glad that we are finally here and on the same page. I wanted to share briefly with you what the Lord has in store for both of you. He intends to use your lives in great ways, but He needed you to pass through this Potter's House to be molded in His likeness and according to what He wants you to become for Him. This chapter of your life will not be easy, not at all, but do not quit before His will is accomplished. He will bless you tremendously for your obedience. He will keep your lives and He will provide for your needs. You are sisters, and soon you will find that you have so much in common. Love and support each other. Barbara, Courtney needs you so much in this country. Be her friend, take good care of her and help her as much as you can."

That was all I needed to hear. I got the affirmation that I wasn't crazy after all, and hadn't made the wrong decision to move back. That super charged meeting left me feeling that I had come full circle.

Everything had fallen into place.

There comes a time when one has to walk alone. Entirely alone. That time is the time when one has to make a decision that will impact the course of their whole life.

Decisions are decisions, whether personal or group but they are decisions. They come with fear, insecurity and faith in the invisible or the unknown. Also, let me tell you something that you might not hear often; when making personal life-changing decisions; listen to yourself, seek advice from the right people but do not let them dictate what you chose for yourself. In the end, you are the one who will live with the consequences of what you have chosen.

In layman terms, life altering decision making taught me this; "Are you willing to bet on God? Are you then willing to bet on yourself?" At the moment, when deciding on one option from the other, it seems like one major door is closing and we are not sure about the other one opening but what we do not know is that this other door that is opening could be the best door that ushers you into your destiny. My decision to return back home seemed like closing one door behind and entering into thousands of others that I was not sure what they would look like but I simply trusted and walked through them.

Throughout my adulthood, I learnt to apply this same lesson over and over again, and I am glad that I have learnt to never allow fear to keep me in limbo..

Chapter Eight

Shaped By Ministry

So often, I've had so many people ask me the same question, "How did you get to become such a good interpreter?" to which I always respond, "It's a long story. How much time do you have to listen to it?" And that story, dear reader began with a book in my hands.

Maranatha Christian Bookstore

A small part of my steadily growing home library; London 2004

One Wednesday afternoon, I was riding the U3 bus from Uxbridge Station to West Drayton where I lived, when I noticed the word, "Maranatha" on the door of a small Christian bookstore near the Uxbridge main roundabout. I was immediately intrigued. The moment I saw it, my heart skipped a beat, and I knew that I had to go there to find out more about it.

The following day, I took time right after classes to search for Maranatha Christian Bookstore. I found it down an alley from the HSBC Bank in Uxbridge, right at the end of the road. I walked in and was warmly greeted by the woody and warm smell of books on the shelves. I felt like a child in a toy store or chocolate factory. In front of me were rows and rows of books of different genres and different shelves of CDs of Christian music and other gifts. I immediately felt like I had reached a place where I belonged. I didn't know why I felt like that, but soon, I was going to find out.

My first purchase was the world acclaimed fiction, "LEFT BEHIND" by Tim LaHaye and Jerry Jenkins. I finished reading the book in three days and knew that I had to go back for more. That marked the beginning of a deeper thirst and understanding of the scriptures through the wealth of different published books.

For the five years that I lived in the UK, I read over two hundred books on different topics, mostly Christian centred.

In that period, I became filled with a recurring sense of urgency, of deep need to learn and it always felt as though the knowledge I was soaking in would be needed, and very soon. I didn't know why, but I always felt like I didn't have much time and had to use the little time granted to learn as much as I could.

So, each time that I got my government income support, as little as it was, I bought at least a book a week. I would have a book on the bus to college, and on the train to church. I allowed myself to get lost in the pages and in so doing, my mind and heart were fed. This increased my knowledge on so many levels and set me up in the place where God wanted me to be for what was about to happen in my life.

A torn piece of paper

In 2007, I was in Rwanda for the Africa Arise conference, where I served as an interpreter alongside Bishop Mukwiza for some sessions. I did not work with Apostle Gitwaza until one Sunday morning when his usher walked to my seat out of nowhere and told me that he needed me to prepare myself because I was going to interpret for him and there couldn't have been any worse timing.

That Sunday was a difficult one for me. Even though I had prepared myself and made it to church, I was extremely sad. Mama was down with an illness and it weighed heavily on my soul. She was deteriorating every single day, and it felt as though she was dying right before my eyes. The pain she suffered had left an indelible scar in my soul, and to make matters worse, my prayers for her healing were not answered. I felt shattered.

I got ready to go to church and I had so many questions for God.

"God, why would you bring me back to see my mother die?" "God, why would you bring me back when I haven't even accomplished much with my life to make her proud?" "Why would I come to see pain that I can't take away?" "Why even bother to pray when you will not do anything about it?" I went to church sad with my many unanswered questions and anger towards this God who, in His Sovereignty, didn't owe me answers.

During that particular service, in the praise and worship, and the church announcements, I was absent-minded. I was only there to tell God that my life was shattered, that Mama was passing away and that there was nothing I could do about it. I was there to tell God that I was tired! Very emotionally tired. I was lost in thought when Yves Mugisha, Apostle Gitwaza's usher came and tapped my shoulder and told me, "Barbara, Apostle has asked me to tell you to get ready to interpret for him!"

Whoah! I was in pain and I wasn't moved at all. As a matter of fact, it didn't mean a lot to me at the moment. In my heart, I was still praying and expressing my sorrow to God. And I got angry. Very angry. My question was; "God, how can you be so unbothered with my heavy heart this morning that you decide to get me up there in front of thousands to preach?"

To be quite honest, nothing made sense to me at that time and interpreting in that church service did not click as a life changing moment for me. Not at all.

I was so unprepared that I had to borrow an English Bible. I used to go to church with a Kinyarwanda Bible since the whole service was done in Kinyarwanda, so I never saw the need to come with an English one. But in this particular service, on that Sunday, for the first time, Apostle Gitwaza went up the stage and I walked behind him.

This was going to happen after a long while since the last interpreter, Pastor James Musoni had stood next to him. No one knew me and I didn't know many people either. I was nervous…very nervous, but I remembered my formula; "Focus on God as the benefactor of your gift."

The first few minutes were light. Apostle has a habit of engaging the audience before going straight to the Word, so that was good to get me comfortable. The comfort didn't last long though, because the moment he shared the title of his sermon, I was shaken! He said that God had told him to speak to people who felt like their lives were in pieces, their hearts broken and their souls crying to God for deliverance. I immediately felt like that was my sermon and one that would feel like a heart surgery. The challenge however, would be to keep it going without losing it in tears.

Apostle Gitwaza even went as far as getting a piece of paper and using it to illustrate what he was talking about. He tore the piece of paper into many pieces and said, "There are lives here that have been torn to a million pieces. You look at those pieces and immediately tell yourself that there is no way I will ever be whole again. But God is doing a new thing in your life. He is collecting the pieces and putting them all back together and refreshing your life." I, on the other hand, wanted to scream. I wanted to just lay myself down and cry. I cried, but in my heart I guess. That was one of the hardest sermons that I ever interpreted, and it will forever be my most memorable one.

I felt seen. God had brought me this far to let me know that He saw me and knew my struggles. My desperation wasn't hidden from Him. That was the first day I stepped on that pulpit to receive my healing, and it was the beginning of a deeper and more beautiful relationship with Him.

Every day that I would stand to serve Him, He would do something wonderful in my soul.

Before thousands

When I started working full time at Zion Temple Kigali in March 2008, I didn't think that interpreting would be part of what I did on a regular basis. I actually didn't do it right away. It was on one random Thursday evening, after working at the church for nearly a month, that Apostle invited me to interpret for him. That Thursday began a journey that lasted many days, countless hours, and a commitment of years to come; to always help people who had trouble understanding the Kinyarwanda sermons.

When I started interpreting, I initially struggled with Bible verses. I will be honest with you. I have failed to memorise entire verses, though I can easily locate them in the Bible. Just don't expect me to unflinchingly recite them for you. Nope. I just know how to find them but will not memorize them. But this is who I have always been, even in school. I am not the memorizing wizard. I simply strive to understand deeply and I am good to go. So, with the Bible, I do not always seek to memorize, though I should, but I seek to understand and live what I have understood.

My lack of memorized Bible verses made my interpretation very hard given that Apostle literally lived in the Bible. This man would read the Bible from 9:00 a.m. when he got in the office, to 3:00 p.m. I was not, and will probably never be a match for that kind of diligent study of the Word. So, seeing that I was weak in the cramming department, I decided to read the scriptures as much as I could when I got home. My reason for this was to gain general knowledge of what those passages meant…not the details.

I remember Apostle Gitwaza often telling me, "The congregation loves your accent, but I know that you don't read your Bible as deeply and as often as you should. Your memory and capacity to summarise what I say saves you every day but you need to grow in the knowledge of the Word." I never argued back. That was the truth. I was going to let my brain and mouth push me and the rest would follow. I grew to become so grateful to the congregation of Zion Temple for enjoying my accent and not paying much attention to my lack of scriptural knowledge.

People have always asked me, "Where do you get the confidence to own that pulpit like you have prepared the sermon with Apostle?" My response has always been simple, "I don't look at the people or pay attention. I simply focus on God not being able to speak Kinyarwanda and needing to fully comprehend the entire message."

You got that right. That's the secret of my trade and the secret behind my success in that area. The moment I walk on the stage, it's not about me, not about Apostle, not about impressing the audience, not about fame but about Him. He has gifted me tremendously, blessed me and equipped me so much for me to focus on anything or anyone else besides Him.

I believe that this is where most of us get it wrong. We forget that for Him we live, by Him we serve, unto Him we minister. The moment we forget this, our downfall has begun.

When I started interpreting, I prayed for the capacity to open my heart and minister from it. Also, I asked God to always connect me to the heart of the preacher that I would be privileged to interpret for. I knew from the beginning that If I wasn't giving from the deepest part of my soul, I would just give plain words. I wasn't by any means the most educated or sharpest person, but I had been given the grace to serve Him in that season and the best way to do it would be from the authenticity of my heart.

This prayer served me well but also worked against me on some days. I observed that on days when my heart was dealing with a specific challenge or issue, it would be so hard for me to really enjoy serving within that context. I would struggle to connect because in those moments, I would be connected to whatever struggle that I would be dealing with. With time, I had to learn to disconnect my emotional struggles from ministry for a given time to get the job done.

To this day, whatever work I do, I do it from the heart, but it's always a challenge to fake "good" when it isn't well with my soul.

Interpreting for Apostle Dr. Paul Gitwaza during Africa Haguruka (Africa Arise & Shine) 2019, at the IPRC Stadium in Kicukiro, Kigali.

ıoment, a lesson

I have served under the leadership of Apostle Gitwaza for some years now, and worked closely with him in different capacities for eleven years and still counting.

I worked as the church secretary, his personal assistant, the Programs Manager and later on the Managing Director at Authentic Radio, the Authentic Prophetic Tours International Coordinator, and Pastor in charge of the church's interpreters. In all these different capacities, I got to know this man in different facets, but I have some common underlying character traits that were crosscutting for me.

First things first; Apostle is a perfectionist. Yes, I have said that, and I am sure that he wouldn't deny it. Everyone who has worked with him will tell you the same. Working with him required going the extra mile, putting in the extra effort and doing your task so well that you left him no room to correct you.

Gosh, I can never forget how many times he had me rewrite letters and print copies because a comma or a full stop was in the wrong place. The pressure to give him correct documents actually turned me into an editor of sorts. Apostle Gitwaza did not preach in English back then, but because he is an ardent reader, his written sermons were always excellent, and he was ready to correct me at any time I missed a point.

To avoid going back and forth with him, I was always determined to bring my A game to whatever it was I would be working on. I guess that's why I worked with him for so long. I pursued excellence because his corrections were tedious. My whole drive was to beat him to it. It was better and less stressful that way. Eventually, when he would have nothing to correct, we would both smile that I would have beaten him at his own perfection game.

As if that wasn't enough to work with, Gitwaza, as so many call him, is a work machine. Let me explain how: back then, he never got tired and sleep was meaningless to him. This is not healthy but he more than once said that it worked for him and that time here on earth was limited compared to the assignments that he had to finish. He did not oblige us to work like that but you would eventually find yourself picking up that kind of pace from him.

He would preach for a whole Sunday; that is; three services (Four hours and thirty minutes in total), do counselling in between the services, leave the church grounds in the wee hours of the morning, and report to work on Monday at 7:00 a.m. and work non-stop. That wasn't even the hardest work he could do. That hardest work title belonged to the overnight services. He would first stand at the pulpit from 9:00 p.m. to midnight of the new year, and then again from 1:00 a.m. to 6:00 a.m.

My God! Who does that? Back in the day when there weren't as many interpreters as there are today, I would stand next to him for those hours too. The only way I endured was by constantly telling myself, "If he can do it, you can do it." By the end of the night, I would head home and take a week off to recover my legs and my voice. I say, "Recover" because I wouldn't feel my legs for two to three days, and my voice would be too hoarse for me to speak. That ministry was intense.

How did I find myself in this position? The first time that I interpreted for a whole overnight service, he called me in his office and told me that we would be standing for long hours, and that I needed to believe that the same God who blessed his resolve to serve wholeheartedly would do the same for me. He often told me that he wasn't special. He was simply unwaveringly committed to what he believed in.

With that in mind, I also had to find the commitment within me to never drop the ball, and in the process, I too was transformed. For as long as the goal was to never drop the ball and keep my eyes focused on God, all would be well.

Learning to be decisive

As a leader, in the different positions that I held and do hold today, one of the most remarkable traits about Apostle Gitwaza is the trust that he bestows in a person when he gives them an assignment. This trait built in me the confidence to be decisive. He never micromanaged me. Instead, he always encouraged me to never allow my fear of failure to keep me stuck in limbo. He believes in taking decisions when needs arise. You might be wrong, and if so, be ready to deal with the consequences instead of simply freezing.

For the two and a half years that I organized and managed tours to Israel, while also managing Authentic Radio, I was often in the deep end of the ocean. But, knowing that I had to lead and decide which way to go kept me focused. Sometimes I made mistakes, but it was better to make them than bury my head in the sand like an ostrich.

Apostle had once told me, "Barbara, life's challenges will never end and they do not disappear either. You have to develop the muscles to solve them without constantly asking me how to do so." I developed those muscles and I am now a firm believer that with God and a consistent drive to break through ironclad walls, one eventually finds solutions.

Trust Issues

Although Apostle is such a perfectionist, he is not perfect. As a matter of fact, he is just as human as we all are. So, did I only learn from his strengths? No...Not at all. Actually, one of the toughest lessons that I learned was from watching him go through unbearable pain because of mistakenly trusting people. In the end, one of the greatest gifts that he gave to people; trust; also worked against him. Apostle Gitwaza gave too much benefit of the doubt to people who in the end revealed that they were not all that they seemed to be. That would require a whole book on its own to explain what I mean.

Unfortunately, this lesson left me with so much disappointment in church leaders and trust issues that instead of my mind set to "Innocent until proven guilty," I always think, "Guilty until proven innocent."

Yes. I am very skeptical and untrusting, but I am working on it. Hopefully, by the time this book is published and in your hands, I will be in a better place to see less guilt and more innocence in people.

A friend in need

Once I started ministering in public for months on end, one thing was apparent to me; I was going to need wardrobe changes to always appear appropriate to meet the kind of work that I did. This was a big challenge for me since I wasn't making a lot of money working at church.

During a church service in Zion Temple Celebration Centre – Gatenga, with my friend in need, Angelique Uwamaliya.

One Sunday morning at church, I whispered to God, "You know that you brought me this far and exposed me greatly. I was fine living under a rock but you chose otherwise. You know that I need to look as smart as the work I do calls me to be. You also know how much money I make. It isn't a salary per se, but an honorarium. I need you to step in and take care of my wardrobe. I am not a beggar and this is your work. I trust you to get this covered."

God heard that prayer and brought a sweet soul in my life that I will forever be grateful for; Angélique Uwamariya. This lady, who was also my colleague and fellow interpreter, had and still has a tailoring business. She always looked great when she came to church, and I always found myself complimenting her on her looks. One day, I complimented her and she looked back at me and smiled. She told me, "You know, I feel like the Lord has been telling me to dress you up. I will make some outfits for you. If you like them, we can keep working together. You do not have to pay me, and even for future clothes you will have your own special prices, which you'll pay at your pace. Let this be my way of serving the Lord."

Lo and behold, the two outfits that she made for me had me looking like a top leading CEO on the cover of a business magazine. I immediately knew that this was going to be a long lasting relationship. Ange, as I fondly call her, has gone from dressing me to designing dresses that fit my shape and match my skin tone, getting me makeup, advising me on what to wear depending on the event I will be attending, to teaching me a lot about fashion and design.

People walk up to me and tell me that they love how I carry myself and how appropriately I dress, and it makes me smile. I smile because I have a friend turned sister who devoted herself to ensuring that I always look my best in public. Because of that, there is no memoir on Barbara without a chapter on Angélique.

God proved to me on so many occasions that He had everything worked out, down to the smallest detail. Think about it, an ordinary woman like me has a stylist that God single-handedly brought into my life. Isn't He amazing? When you give God your very best and a committed 'YES', rest assured that there will be so many Angéliques along your path.

She is definitely his mistress

When I started working in church, it was on an empty slate. Yes, in London I was involved in ministry work, but not on a full time or employee basis. I wasn't aware of what it implied to work in a church environment. To even complicate matters, I was the first face that people saw when entering the church reception. Amongst other things, I also served as the church receptionist, receiving different kinds of people, taking in phone calls and much more.

One of my first challenges was to set my mind on understanding that people came to church for healing. Everyone was sick in their own way, needing the Savior's touch despite pretending to be fine and spiritual. Further, these dear people all came to church hoping to find healing on the very same day that they came for it. In most cases, they also believed that the pastors available were their keys to that healing. If it so happened that they didn't get who they wanted and when they wanted them, they would leave even more hurt, which was oftentimes heartbreaking for me since I would be the one also delivering the bad news.

On top of all that, being an interpreter had its set of challenges that I had to overcome on a daily basis. There were so many expectations on me that I had to take a lot of time to pray and ask for grace, wisdom and favor to meet those expectations, and God surely came through for me. Every time that I stood before the thousands and let Him cover me and use me for Himself, it went so well. He blessed me, but not everyone saw it like that.

I became a victim of malicious slander, and mostly from fellow believers who spread the gossip beyond our church's walls. It is with great shame that I write this, that fellow brothers and sisters in Christ instigated and enjoyed spreading rumors that I was having an affair with Apostle Gitwaza. I recall hearing for the first time, those rumors in 2010, but with each passing year, these rumors grew to more than just rumors.

I figured, if, by God's grace, I got to do my job excellently, remained reliable and a great team member on the church staff, it would all pass. Unfortunately, it didn't pass. To my dismay, the reasoning that quite a number of members of the church and beyond our church community had was that, there was no way Apostle and I could work together so well without any sexual relationship, and thus my "affair" became front page news to whoever was willing to sit and listen. It reached a point where some people viciously made it their life assignment to destroy my marriage, constantly seating my husband to tell him exactly how I was supposedly cheating on him.

I had to, each day, resolve to not pay attention to those rumors. I knew why I was in full time ministry. I was on a mission and on an agreement with God and I wasn't planning on letting slander deter me in any way. I never took any of it seriously...until one evening when I met it carefully described in an online magazine.

In the Media

My father was in a bar where people were talking about an article that had been published, saying how Apostle Gitwaza slept in a coffin and how I was having an affair with him. Alongside the article was a selfie that he and I had taken together in one of our tours in Israel. Papa called me, sounding worried and embarrassed, and asked me to visit him so that we would talk about it, and I accepted. I visited him and we sat and talked.

In his own way, he asked me what I thought about the rumours, and I told him that they were just rumours and he had nothing to worry about. He asked me how I was going to handle people talking about me in that sense, and I laughed. I wasn't guilty, so, what people said about me didn't really matter. What mattered was my relationship with God and my husband and as long as those relationships were intact, nothing else really mattered.

Papa then proposed that I quit my job and reduce my visibility, saying that maybe the noise would die down and get people to forget about me. But, I'm not the type to quit. I was at Zion Temple and in ministry for a reason and a season, and would only quit when the same God who told me to drop everything in London to return to Rwanda showed up and told me to move on again. Up until then, I had never received such directives from God. So I stayed put.

That decision didn't help much though, my unwillingness to run was taken as a justification of the rumours and supposedly proved that my "love" for Apostle Gitwaza was strong enough for me to put my reputation into question. The chatter never stopped and it eventually grew to affect my personal life, opening doors for unwanted issues in my marriage.

All I could do was focus on God, and try to protect myself and my family to the best of my ability.

17th December 2011

My journey in the ministry came full circle on the day that I was ordained as a Pastor on the 17th December 2011. I was ordained a Pastor at the age of 25 years. To be quite honest, I was taken aback by this decision by our church leadership for so many reasons. I didn't feel sure that I had the heart for it. I always felt like there would be a time for me to step out of full time ministry and do something else. Something impactful and transformational but not church based. At the time, I just didn't know what exactly.

When Apostle and the other church leaders informed me and the cohort of ministers who had been chosen for this honorable calling, we all felt scared and not sure in some sense but again, none of us refused to be ordained. It was daunting but it felt right.

I was heavily pregnant and uncomfortable in that ordination but it nonetheless felt special and divine. I remember taking advantage of that moment and praying for my son and asking God to lay a special anointing on my child. Later on, as he grew, I saw the fruits of that prayer.

Being ordained as a Pastor did not change much for me since I had been in full time ministry for a while now but it felt like a deeper validation and an official appointment for my Kingdom duties.

As you hold this book in your hands or on the tablet and read this, you ask yourself, "How did you manage to live your life as a young person yet with such a great calling?"

To be quite honest, I still ask myself the same question every day. I do not have a smart and spiritually deep or even prophetic answer to give you. But I can tell you one thing, I always put authenticity in all that I do and with that same drive, I approached my duties as the Pastor in charge of the Interpreters in Zion Temple Celebration Centre. I have never been one to sugarcoat anything and I have always sought to help people in truth. That same mantra is what I use as a Pastor; fully acknowledging that I am human too, with struggles and battles like everyone else but with a special grace to forego my own sufferings to help a person in need.

Looking back now, I see that one of the greatest tools that God used to shape and mold me into the person that I am today was Ministry. Full time church ministry. Wheewh!!! A journey not for the faint hearted but a revolutionary journey for the bold and humble. Ministry humbled me. Ministry brought me to my knees. Ministry taught me the essence of prayer and the use of that key to survive. Now, don't get me wrong, you might learn these values from other work places but I will tell you this; working in a church environment is a life and universe on its own.

I have learnt that, in any given place that you find yourself serving, the best principle is to make that work count; for yourself, for God and for the people that you serve. We need God to put His anointing over us so that all that we do will be blessed, even if not church related.

The assignment might be difficult or even easy but, like I did and still do; I learnt to approach it with this longing; that in the end; the Lord will look at me and say; "Well done, good and faithful servant."

Chapter Nine

Shaped By Failed Marriage

I have always loved music. I don't know if it has something to do with the way I was raised and the presence of music of different genres in our home, but my soul has always had a thing for music. As a teenager, prior to receiving Christ in my life, I loved spending time listening to RnB and Hip Hop. I knew the lyrics of the songs I watched on DSTV (cable TV) down to the last word, even though I didn't understand much of them.
In the UK, two of my first purchases after I had settled were a small SONY CD Player and a Walkman. If I wasn't reading a book while riding the bus or train, I would be listening to music. Music was an escape to a wonderful land of soothing melodies that calmed my spirit.

When I made my shift to Rwanda and returned to church, one of the greatest moments in our services for me was the slot given to Praise and Worship, which gave me a platform to come to God bare and truthful to myself and to Him, and the church band, Asaph Music International created that environment for me. Every time I entered church, my spirit was drawn to them simply because they provided me with a deep connection to God.

Soon enough though, I came to love more about Asaph than just their melodies.

More than melodies

Denis Dadou Habumugisha, a worship leader and one of the best acoustic guitarists I have ever met, was the leader of Asaph Music International and also worked in the Compassion Rwanda church office.

He was a friend to my direct supervisor, the church Administrator, Mashimango Bénédiction who was also a musician and singer in Asaph.

Dadou always came to see Mass, as we like to call him, in his office, where Mass would tease him and tell him that it could work out between us if we dated. I never took Mass seriously because he was such a joker and I wasn't interested in dating a church guy I worked with. To me, Dadou was on the fast track to becoming a pastor, and I had pledged to never marry one.

I knew that I was going to be in ministry full time and felt that I needed balance, meaning a man who didn't work in the church administration. But, the connection happened. As I reminisce and write about this, I have a smile on my face. Mass couldn't give up!

One Friday afternoon, I asked Mass for a ride home from church. Unbeknownst to me, Dadou would also be riding with him that day. On the way, we talked and joked, and I must have caught Dadou's attention and interest, because he looked at me and told me, "We'll finish this conversation au tour d'un verre (over a drink)."

In his unique way, he had just asked me out on a date. However, he never mentioned it again in the following weeks that passed. I, out of curiosity, eventually had to ask him what happened to the au tour d'un verre. Rest assured dear reader that I had no shame in asking him about that au tour d'un verre. Listen, I had come to like him, and found his introverted demeanor quite intriguing. He was different from all the other guys who had asked me out before, but we were not getting to that au tour d'un verre soon enough. Hahahaha! Well, we eventually got to it.

He called me after another few weeks and proposed that we go out for dinner at Chez John - Kiyovu, which is one of my favorite restaurants in Kigali. We had a great evening there. The conversation was light and I loved being in his presence. He expressed his interest in dating me and I told him that I was going to think about it. I liked him, but I still felt that he was eventually going to be a pastor, and I also knew that Christians mostly didn't date just for dating.

There was always the final destination in mind; marriage. To me, that meant that if I decided to date him, I'd have to do so with marriage in mind, and I wasn't sure if I was ready for that life.

Nonetheless, the date ended so well. I had so much fun and I left with a sense of having made a connection to a church guy who wasn't what I expected him to be.

In the following week, Dadou got a job at one of the commercial banks in Kigali and had to travel to Nigeria for a six-month training. He left before we had something solid going on besides the friendly text messages or phone calls. As immature as I was, I hastily made up my mind based on my assumptions and fears that it wouldn't work for the both of us, and what did I do? I turned down his "proposal" via email. Savage, I know, but I wasn't going to keep him waiting for all those months. I closed that file and moved on.

The calm to my storms

In the course of the next six months, I stayed in touch with Dadou, despite the email I had sent him. I would occasionally send him a text message to check on him and make sure that we stayed in touch. Don't ask me why, but for some reason, I didn't want to completely cut off communication with him. Gracefully, he too remained in touch, and with time, I began to feel like I had rushed to refuse his request and maybe something could have worked out between us.

When he finished his training course in Nigeria and returned to Rwanda, I started seeing him more often than before. Every Monday, Wednesday and Friday evenings, we would meet when he came to church for choir practice. With time, I began to feel comfortable and serene around him that I found myself always looking forward to seeing him.

Slowly, I started to develop feelings for him without knowing it. I always caught myself pointlessly thinking of him, and sometimes, I would actually go to town and check on him in his office.

I always made it a point to check on him in his office every time that I went to town and whenever he saw me, he would just laugh. He found these random "check-ins" crazy and I didn't care. I liked him, so why did I have to pretend that I didn't like him? Where was that going to get me? I embarrassed myself so many times but I didn't really care. If he was liked so much, he had to be shown that. Full stop.

Our friendship grew and we decided to start dating on 23rd July 2009 to see where things between us would go with time. It didn't take long before we knew that we wanted to spend the rest of our lives together, and Dadou proposed with a ring one evening when we had gone out with friends, and sang a song for me. Yes, during our relationship, I knew that we were heading towards marriage, but that gesture warmed my heart on so many levels. It was nothing fancy…just a simple evening with friends, a ring and a song, and I was set to marry this quiet man that I had crossed paths with.

We then spent the upcoming months meeting family members, introducing our plans for marriage and getting ready for not only our wedding, but also our married life together.

We didn't know how time passed by so fast and we tied the knot on the 23rd July 2011, on the same day two years later, that we made our commitment to date. We became husband and wife, and we were married…for nine years.

Misconceptions

Growing up, when I thought of marriage, it had to be with a God-loving man and he absolutely had to be a member of Zion Temple. Why, you wonder. Let me explain. It was in this church that my life had been transformed. It was also in this church that I learnt so much that shaped me to become the young woman that I was. It is where I acquired communication skills, where I learned to speak confidently in public, where I mastered the art of networking, where I became wise and much more.

It was also where I saw all that God had accomplished with Apostle Gitwaza and how many lives that his spiritual leadership had transformed, and that always made me wonder, "What can I accomplish standing next to him?" Yes, you got that right, I am an ambitious woman and at the back of my mind, I always wondered what more could this opportunity and platform give me? It's here that I always knew that I would get the specific blessings and promises made by God to me years back while living in London and since I have that conviction, I knew that Zion Temple was where I needed to be for a long while. I also felt like I needed a man specifically from that church to facilitate me in that pursuit.

So, when Dadou and I got married, I was committed to making his life much better and thought that together as a team, we would be unstoppable.

I thought that if he loved me and I respected him, we were good to go. I thought that as long as we shared the same faith and had common backgrounds, we were compatible. I thought, if we attend the church, my dreams in clear sight, his dreams in the corporate world pursued, we could make it in both worlds. How wrong I was.

Very immature way of looking at marriage. Marriage is more than your ambitions, more than your dreams. Marriage is life. Marriage is your capacity to make it work between you two without anyone losing their mind in the process. The rest is additional. But I didn't know any of that. I was in for a rude awakening.

For starters, our marriage became a platform for self-discovery, and one of the key revelations that I had throughout the years, was the understanding of what authenticity looked like for me, what I wanted to do with my life and where I wanted to go. I started discovering what I liked and didn't like, and these discoveries only served to bring friction and frustration in our household.

I was frustrated to realise that I am a go getter, but wasn't often encouraged to...well...go get it. I was frustrated to realise the kind of treatment I needed as a woman, but didn't receive. And unfortunately, this truth only served to enlarge the already existing gaping distance between me and my partner.

I needed a man who would support my passion and talents, and understand why I was in full time ministry at the time. I needed someone who would still encourage me to pursue my dreams even though I was still in ministry. I needed someone who would understand me, encourage me and empower me to be the best version of myself.

I was never physically abused, but tons of emotional distress made up for it. What I craved and lacked got me to a point where I almost completely lost my mind.

Lord, help me find my car

Over the course of time, I developed severe anxiety and started having panic attacks. I didn't know it at the time and I couldn't understand what was happening to me. I had been depressed for such a long time that it took me a while to acknowledge that I even had a problem.

I put it all on God with prayer, and the Holy Spirit did help me through it, but I also needed professional help at the time.

I would wake up in the middle of the night feeling like I couldn't breathe, and I also had constant migraines that I always had medication for. It worsened as I didn't deal with it, to the point I would park my car and forget where I left it. This happened three times, and the anxiety I would get in the parking lot was unbearable.

One of those times, I was coming from an intense high profile meeting in which I had worked as an interpreter. My brain battery was already low before I went to that event, but I still had to do my job. I remember praying, "Holy Spirit, you know my mind is not right these days, but I need the money and I need to live. If this gig doesn't go through, I'll never be called for another one. Take over and make sure I get it right." With that, I did an awesome job and got congratulated by many. But at the end of the event, as I walked out to the parking lot, I couldn't remember where I parked my car…again.

My brain battery was completely dead at this point. All I could do was survive on prayer. So I uttered, "Lord, if you love me, help me find my car," and sure enough, He helped me find it but the anxiety that I felt in those minutes that I spent searching for my car was just too much. In the car, as I sat to catch my breath, I realized that my mind was slipping away, and I knew then that I couldn't keep fighting my soul. I had to do something at this point. I had already compromised my emotions and my heart to make my marriage work, but I wasn't going to let go of my mind. That was it for me. I made the decision to stand up for myself.

A week later, the anxiety didn't stop but only kept getting worse. At times I felt like my heart was about to burst out of my chest. I went to see a doctor. As he examined me, he asked if my work or my home were stressing me out. I identified that it was home and as I described what was happening to me, he determined that I was having panic attacks. He told me that I was young and I shouldn't have to allow too much stress to that point. He then explained to me that if my marriage caused stress, panic attacks were bound to be triggered by anything.

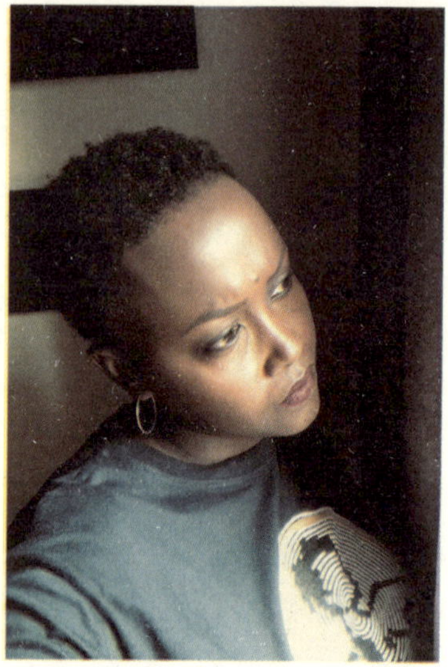

Going through my divorce with a burdened heart and an unstable mind, I couldn't stop thinking about how I had ended up there, with shattered dreams.

Since there is a history of blood pressure, diabetes and cancer in my family, the doctor told me that I was prone to get either of them if I was to stay in such a marriage. He explained to me that I ended up in his office because my body was rejecting the coping mechanisms that I had developed, and that I had to seek professional help. He prescribed me anti-depressants that were meant to help me calm down but also give me some good sleep.

He advised against getting counseled by a pastor and told me to go to a trained psychologist equipped to help me carry the weight. Now this was funny. Clearly he didn't know that I was a pastor and I liked it. He could help without any bias or any judgement. This doctor told me that I needed someone to talk to about what I was going through, and therapy would either restore my marriage or get me out of it. Either way, it would help me one way or another.

Apart from the doctor recommending therapy, a friend of mine, Natacha had also been trying to convince me that I needed counselling, since way before I realized that I needed it. She had taken a six-month Lay Counselling course at Lighthouse Counselling & Training Center, Rwanda. At the time she was taking it, me and a group of her friends always made fun of her. We were those people who still had the stigma that mental health issues were white people problems. Well, she must have had the last laugh when I ended up seeking therapy from Lighthouse.

I got a counsellor there, and in our first session, I told her all about my anxiety and panic attacks and that I wanted her to advise me on how to fix my marriage to which she clarified that, that's not how therapy worked. She pointed out that I was there because I was not fine and I needed to work out my issues. This process would either make things better or move me to the point of deciding what to do with my life.

More than once, I asked her how I could stay married, and she always answered that she would guide me to make my own decisions rather than make them for me. In one of the sessions, she gave me an assignment. She asked me to write down a list of pros and cons of staying married, and what my life would look like in a year if I stayed married or got a divorce. She told me that this would help me process my thoughts on my marriage and probably help me come up with a decision that I was fine with. It took me a whole two weeks to work on that list. I was scared that if I wrote it down and read it to myself, I would have to make the hard decisions that I didn't want to make, and eventually that's what happened.

I read my list and realized that I would benefit more if I walked away from the marriage. Reading it frightened me, because in my mind, there was no way I was getting a divorce. But over time, so much happened in my marriage that made me realise that it wasn't mentally healthy for me to stay.

Ni ko Zubakwa

Being born and raised Rwandan comes with great DOs and grave DON'Ts when it comes to marriage, and divorce is one of the latter. Our Rwandan culture even has proverbs and sayings centered on staying married. One of the common ones is, NI UKO ZUBAKWA (That's how marriages are built). This simply means that marriage is difficult but that's how it has always been done by the generations of our grandmothers, mothers and aunties.

So as my marriage was slowly crumbling beneath my feet, I was faced with two options; abandon my authentic self because NI UKO ZUBAKWA, or love myself enough to live in my truth and pursue the path I was destined to walk. I chose the latter. Now, do not get me wrong. This self-love that I am talking about is not from a selfish standpoint, but from a place of understanding that if I didn't live from the heart, I would literally die.

Again, after "KUBAKA (building)" for nine years, I couldn't just simply wake up and walk away. It wasn't a decision to take lightly. It took me a number of months to think about it, and the prospect of such a daunting and frightening decision required me to be sure that accepting this path was what was right.

I considered how the Rwandan society wouldn't be kind or understanding. I thought of the labelling that would come with it and I knew that it wouldn't end there. I knew that I would be an outcast in some way and not only was it going to have a certain effect on my life, but would forever affect my children in a way that their father and I would have to find a way to manage it.

Push came to shove and I knew that I had to do it. The process itself was emotionally painful and exhausting. I had to keep checking myself to see if I was fine in my skin, in my right mind, and not acting out of anger but from conviction. It was a weary and hard decision.

I decided to walk away from my marriage because I felt like I was losing my mind, and I couldn't afford that because my mind is one of my most precious possessions. I couldn't work or be a parent for that matter without it, I couldn't function professionally, and I wasn't going to raise my children as a mentally unstable mother just for the sake of pleasing the society.

Mixed Feelings

Marriage is a beautiful thing. It's the first institution that God established; proof that He knew so well that neither a man nor a woman were meant to be alone without such a framework. Yes, I do realise that over the years, commitment and love have taken different forms and shapes but let's not go there now. Let's look at marriage. Marriage is an institution that one should enter in well prepared, well informed and well aware of what is to come. With that, I am not implying that it is all doom. No it isn't. As a matter of fact, it is a mixture of the good and the bad, just like life is, but this time round, you are going through the good and the bad with someone who, it often feels like they are joined to you at the hip. This someone is a person that you didn't grow up together with, do not fully know each other but chose to navigate life together and hope for the happily ever after together.

In hindsight, I would say that I was ill prepared for marriage. My expectations were too rosy, immature and not well defined as they should have been. I was blindsided by my lack of self-understanding, lack of clarity on marriage, and what I really wanted in my life as a person, a partner and in my married life.

Going through separation, divorce and the hurricane that came with it, I was forced to go back to the beginning of the journey and one striking truth that came to me was the understanding that a divorce doesn't start in court, but in most cases, in courtship.

Marriage and divorce in this case; taught me the importance of self-understanding, selflessness and maturity. These three also taught me the importance of knowledge and wisdom in navigating relationships. Now, I am not proclaiming to be the twin sister of King Solomon but again, I will say this; nine years of pursuing and failing to attain "Oneness" with another full grown human being will teach you so much in life.

Boys and Girls, Ladies and Gentlemen, (I smile as I even write this), marriage is a beautiful project. One for those who understand what that commitment implies and who are willing to keep working at it until their happily ever after arrives. Not giving up on each other, not walking away and certainly not allowing life's challenges to deter that commitment.

Chapter Ten

Shaped By Grief

For the entirety of my whole life, my mother was one of the strongest and most resilient woman that I knew. Mama was passionate, independent, such a hard worker and so much more. Laurette lived her life to the fullest. She was always there when I needed her. When I needed a hug, I always got a tight one. When I needed to have a good laugh, she boisterously laughed with me. And, when I needed some money and she had some, best believe that she would cheerfully give me some.

She loved, and she loved hard. In anything that she found herself involved in, you could bet that she would give it more than a hundred percent. She was full of life and she gave life wherever she went. If you met her, her warm soul would not leave you the same way she found you.

I had last seen her healthy in 2002 when we both travelled to Belgium, and for the five years that I lived in London, we only kept in touch through letters, emails, phone calls and photos that people travelling back home would bring me.

Around 2004, she fell ill, and every time we talked on the phone, she made me believe that it wasn't that bad. She didn't want me to worry, given that there wasn't anything that I could do about it. She kept telling me, "Imana izankiza humura (Don't worry. God will heal me)." I believed her and I believed that God would one day miraculously touch and heal her body.

Each day, I prayed for her health. I desperately wanted her to get well, and I couldn't wait for the day that I would get to see her again and just get to enjoy life with her. I missed her terribly as I was growing up into a young woman that needed her so much to navigate through the hurdles of life.

As her condition worsened, Papa decided that the best thing was for him was to take her to Belgium for treatment, which he did in 2006.

Mama stayed in the hospital for sometime, going through extensive testing to find out what she was suffering from. She an was later diagnosed with Sjogren Syndrome, an incurable autoimmune disease that made her immune system attack her own body cells and tissues. Since her condition couldn't be cured, she stayed in Belgium for the fundamental treatments and once all was done, she returned to Rwanda. We didn't know for how long she would be alive, but deep down, we knew that she didn't have much time.

At the time of Mama's return, I was also getting ready to fly back home. I knew that the timing was perfect. I was not only returning for divine purposes, but also for a chance to spend the remaining years of her life at her side. Little did I know that I wasn't ready for what awaited me.

Pain in the eyes

I saw Mama on July 7th 2007, five years after I had last seen her. She had come to the airport with my father to pick me up on the day I returned home.

Coming out of the plane and breathing in my beautiful country's fresh air, I was excited to be back home. I felt wonderful. I felt peaceful. It felt as though a piece of the puzzle of my life had fallen into place. After picking my luggage, I went to the waiting area, where I found Papa waiting for me. I hugged him tight and simply looked at him. We had last met in 2006 when he had come to visit us in London, before going to check on Mama in Belgium. It had been a year since I last saw him.

To my surprise, he was alone. I didn't see Mama next to him and wondered why.

I asked him where she was, and he told me that she wasn't feeling well and that she was in the car waiting for me. We then walked to the car, my heart beating fast, excited to see her.

Strapped in the front seat was Mama patiently waiting for me. I opened the door, expecting her to come out and hug me, but she didn't. I looked at her and froze. Mama had lost so much weight. She looked pale and in pain…not physically, but emotionally. The disease had taken such a toll on her, and it showed. We gazed at each other and I immediately saw the pain in her eyes; pain over her life fading away, pain over the things she couldn't do anymore, like standing up and hugging me. I could see it in her eyes and I immediately felt her heart. Seeing that she couldn't stand to hug me, I slumped down and reached out to hug her in the car. She couldn't hug me back because her arms had also started to get paralyzed, and she teared up as I held her tight. At that moment, I couldn't cry. My heart was frozen and I didn't know how I could express the pain that I felt from finding her in that condition.

No one had told me that she couldn't walk anymore, so I asked Papa why no one had told me about the state she was in, and with sadness, he looked at me and told me that it wasn't as bad as I saw it. That was my cue to not appear alarmed. Mama had enough to deal with than me bringing even more attention to her state.

From the airport, we drove home quietly. Papa tried to have some small talk, asking me how the flight had been, but Mama didn't say much. Her voice and speech had also been affected by the disorder that she suffered from. I was in utter shock. So many thoughts raced in my mind and I instantly felt afraid of losing her.

It would be a few more years before she passed on, but from the look that she gave me in that parking lot, I knew that we would live with death throughout the remainder of her life.

With Mama in her last years alive before she passed on in 2012.

Living with death

As it is with Sjogren Syndrome, the patient loses a piece of life and organ function each day as their healthy cells are attacked and destroyed. Mama wasn't exempted from the ruthlessness of this disease. She lost something each day.

At first, she could walk when held and supported by someone, then her knees gave away eventually and we had to get her a wheelchair. Her speech went from not being heard clearly to not being heard at all. One day she could feed herself, and the next she couldn't. Basically, everything started failing one after the other.

This process went on for five years, and it was extremely hard for Mama, who had always known herself as a vibrant, passionate, independent, charismatic, charming and very beautiful woman. In her condition, slowly eroding each day, she couldn't recognize herself. Mama reached a point where all she could do was look at us and just cry. It was not a way to live and it wasn't the way for her to die either. But, life was what it was.

Every time I looked at Mama, I always remembered the ghastly look that she gave me at the airport when I found her in the car and she couldn't stand up to hug me. The look simply told me, "This is what I have become. I am passing away."

Later on, she opened up and told me, "You will need to be strong and help me through this all."

I realized that she needed me to be the very things that she had always been for me. So, I sucked it in, toughened up and was strong for the both of us and our whole family. I had to find a way to not fall apart, and numbing myself was the only way I knew to do it.

Her pain and her tears broke my heart into pieces each day. Even worse was the fact that I had to be strong for her, for my father and for my brothers. I kept telling myself that I had to keep it together and so I did. I learned to live with the loss of her life yet she was still there with us. I reasoned, "It's not easy for her. She is sick, so let me not think about what her state means to me," but the state she was in killed me.

Her illness took a piece of my innocence and softness as a daughter, and replaced it with bitterness, anger and pain.

"Why can't you heal her, God? Why?" I always asked Him.

"What will my life look like in her absence?" I wondered.

"Why her?"

The 16th & 23rd July 2011

It is every girl's dream to find love and share that experience with the most important woman in her life; her mother. Yes, I found love, but Mama had fallen so ill and life was so tasteless that introducing my fiancé, Dadou, to her wasn't the experience that I had envisioned.

Mama simply looked at him when I brought him home, and sheepishly asked him, "Will you manage my daughter? I raised her. I know how strong-willed and independent she is. Will you manage her?" I was embarrassed, but this was Laurette. I knew she couldn't cut corners with Dadou. He laughed and told her, "Mama, I love her. I will manage."

In hindsight, Mama knew what those years of living alone in England and returning to Kigali only to find her life wasting away done to me. She knew, more or less what it would take a man who would marry me.

All I knew was to be strong, tough, and survive, on the other hand, love required of me vulnerability and trust, attributes that I would need to cultivate over time. It was going to be a long soul-searching journey that required resilience.

After that introduction, we started getting ready for our wedding. To be quite honest, I had mixed feelings over it all. At that point, Mama was bedridden and couldn't attend any of my functions. I didn't understand how I was going to get married in her absence yet she was still alive. It didn't make sense to me at all.

As tradition would have it, my Gusaba (Dowry giving ceremony) was on the 16th July 2011. For that function, as agreed with my parents, we got someone to represent Mama, receive her gift and congratulate us at the ceremony. We got my godmother, Aunt Faith Mamboleo to stand in perform all Mama's duties.

Since the ceremony had been held in a rented venue, at the end, when the guests from the groom's side had left, I got in a car with a cousin of mine and a few friends, and drove home to see Mama. There, we took pictures and she at least got to see me in my sea blue mushanana (Rwandan traditional outfit). She was all dressed up, with some makeup and sat in her wheelchair. When she saw me, she smiled and told me, "Feliçitations (Congratulations)". We hugged and I told her all about the ceremony. She held back her tears thinking she'd ruin my day, and I did the same, thinking I'd break her heart even more. So much was exchanged in our silence and yet not experienced in that fleeting moment.

One week later, it was my wedding day. I had discussed with Dadou that after the church ceremony, we would need to go see Mama and take pictures with her again. I wanted her to see me and my husband. I wanted her to see my gown and check my finger for the wedding band, and in a small way yet paramount, be part of my big day.

After the church ceremony, we went to see her with photographers with our best man and matron. It was emotional for me. I kept telling myself that I had to be grateful to God that she was actually alive and that she got to see me off, married. This thinking kept my tears at bay and Mama did the same as she had done a week before. But it was so hard.

She loved my dress, told me that I looked beautiful and that she was so happy for me. Though she battled her tears, I could see the joy she had behind the well in her eyes. We took our pictures and then made our way back to the venue where the wedding reception was held. As I headed out, I kept wondering, "what's there for me to celebrate if I'm leaving her on that bed?"

I had to muster all the courage that I could find to stay in the blissful moment of celebration of love in her absence.

During the wedding reception, flashes of her in her bed, alone thinking of how she missed my wedding, kept crossing my mind. That reception had me using a lot of mental energy to not think of her absence and her pain

Expected but still painful nonetheless

Right after our wedding, Dadou and I embarked on our married life and God blessed us with the fruit of our womb.

I conceived right away and it wasn't exciting. My first pregnancy was a difficult one. I was constantly at risk of having a miscarriage, and lived in fear of losing my first-born during the first trimester and a half. Still, I always did my best to visit my parents despite my situation.

My hope and prayer was that I could get to deliver my first-born with Mama still alive, because her health was still deteriorating at a faster rate than the previous years.

One evening, when I was six months pregnant, I felt such a great sense of urgency to go and visit her. I drove home and found Mama in the bedroom. I sat in front of the bed feeling exhausted. We sat quietly and then with a soft voice, she asked, "Barbara, umwana ameze ate? (How is the baby doing?)". I told her that I was getting well and eating much better each day, and we were quiet again. In our moment of silence, our hearts communicated loudly like it always felt. All we did was look at each other.

Mama was weary, and even talking was difficult for her at that point. I was tired too with the extra weight that came with the pregnancy, and also emotionally from having watched her struggle and suffer for five years.

As I sat quietly in her silent yet so loud presence, it dawned on me that she was in her final days. I felt it so deeply that the fear of losing her crept up on me again. I couldn't take it anymore, a few minutes later, I got up and told her that it was getting late and I had to leave. She teared up and told me goodbye. This goodbye felt different. Permanent. Heavy. Final.

On the drive home, tears streamed down my cheeks. Mama was going to die soon. I didn't know when, but she was passing soon. As I cried, I also talked to my unborn child, telling him, "This is very hard for me, but please be fine. I don't need you to be unwell. Just be fine for me while I handle this loss."

When I got home, I couldn't eat or talk much. My heart had sunk in a hole and I didn't know when it would surface again. I went to bed early but couldn't sleep. I kept tossing and turning until my husband finally came to bed. As we slept, he sensed that I wasn't fine. He held me and asked me, "Baby, are you fine?"

With that question, I burst out crying. "Mama is dying soon and I don't know if I will survive it. I can't survive her death while pregnant," I told him, heartbroken. He comforted me and told me that I would be well. And after a few more hours of crying, I was finally able to fall asleep.

You have to be strong

Mama fell sick and came down with a fever on the Sunday evening of the 6th February 2012, and she was taken to King Faisal hospital. I went to visit her on Monday morning. She was so weak and frail, but at that moment, I chose to not think that she was actually going to pass away that week.

On Tuesday, I also returned to check on her. Deep in my heart, I was conflicted. I knew that she'd pass away at any time, but I also prayed that she lived longer. I wanted her to be there when I had my first-born. I wanted her to hold him, kiss him and know that her blood was flowing in the veins of my little bundle of joy. But then, it felt selfish of me to wish for her to live longer in pain. So I was confused.

I went to work on Wednesday morning. At around 11:30 a.m., Bishop Mukwiza's wife, Pastor Consolée Mukwiza and another church member, Christian Ibambasi, found me at the reception. She asked me to go to town with them to visit a shop, and I obliged. We went to a shop called Chez Angélique and as soon as we entered, I sat down and Pastor Consolée went back outside to answer a phone call.

Unbeknownst to me, Mama had passed away in those hours and my husband had traced my whereabouts and called Pastor Consolée and Christian asking them to take me back to the church. Pastor Consolée came back to the shop with a changed demeanor and I immediately felt it. Mama was gone.

I asked her immediately, "Is Mama dead?" to which she denied, telling me that there was nothing wrong but we had to quickly go back to church. I knew it, and I kept asking them if Mama was alright, to which Christian said, "Don't worry, your mother is fine. We just have to quickly go back to church."

Despite their efforts to appear normal, my heart told me otherwise. It was sure and certain that there was a piece of me that had just left this world. Everything else being told to me was just a way of leading me on for the sake of keeping me safe in my state as a pregnant mother.

We got to the church, where I found my husband waiting for me. I looked at him and asked him, "Mama yapfuye (Has Mama died)?" and he told me that she had passed but that he needed me to sit down. It didn't register in my mind that she had passed. As we entered the administration wing of the church building, we were rushed to Apostle's office. Reaching there, we found him with Bishop Charles Mudakikwa. I could tell by the look on his face that telling a 7-months pregnant woman about the passing of her mother was not something he was used to.

Apostle asked us to sit down and we did. He then looked at me and told me, "Barbara, I am so sorry for your loss. Pastor Dadou just communicated to me that your mother has rested. I wanted you both to come so that we pray. She is resting and in a better place." It all felt unreal. I was quiet and trying to process everything at the moment. Apostle prayed for me and we left his office. My husband was worried for me and acted like he was carrying a basket of eggs while walking on a heap of hot coal. I understood him but that wasn't my main concern at that moment.

I felt like I had somehow grieved Mama's loss in advance, on the night that I had visited her and cried my heart out in my bed. At that moment, I didn't feel like a basket of eggs, but rather a ravenous Mama bear. I was starving. I was pregnant and craving something to eat. That's all that mattered before we went to see Mama at the hospital. I pestered my husband and Mary, an old childhood friend of mine, to get me something to eat, and so we stopped at a snack shop and got some samosas and juice. Once I had eaten, I felt much better and we drove to the hospital.

Arriving there, we walked to the room where Mama had spent her last hours. I found my father and aunties there, all in tears. When they saw me, they all shifted their attention to me and started telling me, "Ihangane. Bibaho mu buzima (Be strong. That's life)." By "Be strong," they inadvertently communicated to me to hold in my tears.

King Faisal Hospital rooms have a balcony. At that moment, I felt like I needed to breathe before anything else; so, I walked out from the room and stood at the balcony. I needed to gain the strength to go and see Mama, who at this moment was covered up by a white sheet. A few minutes later, I went back inside and went by her bed. As I approached her, I kept telling myself, "She is resting." I stood in front of her bed and rolled away the bedsheet and right then, I felt numb. I felt dead. I felt my body go cold, then warm again, and back to cold again. I also felt confused. Mama was gone. Serene, as though sleeping, her fair skinned face shrunken, she lay there, no longer with us.

My husband held my hand and told me, "Sorry. I am so sorry."

I looked at Mama and felt sad…sad that she was gone…and sad that she left without ever getting to hold her first grandchild. I couldn't dare process any more of my feelings, so I slowly covered her face again and walked out again to the balcony. There, my father and my husband came to me and told me, "Ihangane (Be strong)."

"What am I to do?" I thought. "Do I even have a choice? To mourn? To cry?" For the sake of saving my baby from going into distress, I couldn't. It was hard. It was heart-wrenching. I was also afraid of crying because I felt like if I did, I would never stop. I felt like I would cry for every single day that she died in front of my eyes, from the first day that I saw the pain in her beautiful big brown eyes at the airport to that very moment of covering her face again with that white bedsheet.

I decided to numb myself again. It was what I did best. Numbing was and had always been my coping mechanism. Unhealthy, I know, but numbing had kept me going for some time. It surely wasn't going to disappoint me in my time of greatest need. Despite my numbness, however, I still felt like I carried a rock on my heart, so heavy that it often felt like I couldn't breathe. Throughout the mourning period and the burial ceremony, I carried it, never shed a tear, and pushed on each day.

Up until today, when I think of my mother's death, I also think of my son's birth. It's a complex feeling, a juxtaposition of grief and joy…one that I will always walk with for the rest of my life.

The years 2007 - 2012 were intense for me. Returning to Rwanda to find my mother ill, taking care of her, loving her through both her pain and mine, and experiencing her slow death each day was much more than heeding the call of God for my life. I reckoned that it was also His gift of time offered to me. God wanted to give me my mother's last years on this earth with her, to make fresh memories and learn the final lessons on womanhood and motherhood from her.

Those years, although painful, I cherish every day.

On another note, grief is such a heavy emotion to bear. To this day, I have only come to reach this conclusion that grief should be allowed space to be experienced. One should give themselves the gift to feel that pain of loss, cry their tears and bury their dead in peace.

The loss of my mother at such a delicate time never gave me the time and means to grieve and over the years, I had to teach myself to find little courage to visit those memories and allow myself to feel the pain here and there but not long enough to break the wall around my heart.

It was during the time of writing this chapter, one of the hardest chapters for me to write in this book that I finally let go and cried for her death. Not pregnant. Not afraid. Not confused. Cried. Let it all out. I mourned for the grandsons that she never met. The accomplishments of the daughter that she raised that she never enjoyed and the future that I am yet to see, that I strongly believe will be a bright one.

Dear reader, I realized that grief had shaped me into an emotionless soul. Pain wasn't welcome. Joy was half lived. I was a captive, until SHAPED came along and ordered me to write about this great loss.

I pray that you find the courage to cry over what you have lost.

Chapter Eleven

Shaped By Motherhood

After the lloss of my mother, my mind was constantly troubled with the whole concept of motherhood, since I was about to be one. First of all, I didn't really grow up around babies, so I didn't know how to carry, wash and even feed one. One of the babies that I recall holding and taking care of was Deborah Ineza, Félin and Josée Gakwaya's firstborn, since then, I had not come across infants.

Secondly, I didn't feel adequately equipped to be a mother. I believed that one needed to have their mother alive to teach them everything they needed to know about motherhood. Mine had just passed away and I had no idea how to navigate this new journey I was about to embark on.

Thirdly, I was worried that I was not good enough to handle the heavy responsibilities that came with raising children. God had trusted me and my ex-husband to uniquely shape the kids He blessed us with into good people, outstanding citizens, and blessings to their families, the nation and the body of Christ. All these thoughts, coupled with grief, got me anxious. Thankfully, God had everything planned, and I was about to discover one of my greatest blessings.

A God-given mother

Shortly after the death of Mama, I had my firstborn son, with the special care and assistance of maternal cousin, Pastor Assumpta and her husband, Pastor François Bayingana.

On the day that I delivered my son, I was with Assumpta, and was later joined by Alice Kakule, my maid of honor who was heavily due herself. I will always be grateful for her sacrifice that day and night. She waited on me to give birth until she couldn't anymore and had to return home to rest. I was in labor for so long, a day and a half but when it was time, Assumpta tirelessly encouraged me to push until my child was born at 3 a.m. on a Sunday morning.

Since I didn't even know how to hold a baby, and was always afraid that if I tried to wash one, he would fall from my hands and drown in the basin and die, Assumpta didn't make fun of me, and instead showed me how it was done the first time I had to wash my son. She simply held Koen, showed me how to wash him for three days, and I was set.

My next challenge was to make that tiny human burp, which I'm still terrible at. Believe me when I say that burping is a science on its own! I can breastfeed and wake up five times in the night...but burping torments me. Thank God for Assumpta though, and her super powers. Every time she held my little boy, he burped effortlessly and went to sleep.

I on the other hand stayed awake most nights because I never got my burping game on point. With new motherhood, I always wondered why no one ever prepared me with baby know how. Babies love waking up in the middle of the night, screaming on top of their lungs. To this day, I do not know why they do that. These little humans bully young mothers like no other force known to mankind! Or maybe it was just my boys who chose to teach me motherhood the hard way.

Assumpta also taught me how to sneak out on a sleeping baby to grab a quick shower or meal before he woke up. She'd hold my son for hours while I caught some sleep and she always made sure that in the night, before going to bed, she would make me a hot bowl of healthy porridge to eat when I woke up to breastfeed.

My introduction to motherhood wasn't easy but through Assumpta's precious life, God showed me that though I had lost my biological mother, I had another mother to birth me into motherhood.

Mother to sons

Koen (meaning Priest) Rey (meaning King) Habumugisha (meaning Where there is a blessing in Kinyarwanda) is my firstborn son. Born on the 6th May 2012. An old soul from the time he was conceived. Very introspective, observant and analytical. His pregnancy, as mentioned earlier, had its challenges linked to the death of my mother that affected me in so many ways but his birth brought healing in my life. To this day, Koen is the calm in our vibrant household. Yes, the combination of me and Keshawn, his brother, creates such a vibrancy, that we need to have

Koen around to balance us out.

Today, when I look at him, I remember the prayers that I prayed for him and how God answered each one of them. His love for God and desire to see Him is one thing that always assures me. His hunger for Him will never leave him unsatisfied.

The pregnancy that gave me Keshawn (meaning God is gracious) Rapha (meaning Healer) Habumugisha (meaning Where there is a blessing in Kinyarwanda) born on the 12th November 2017, my second born son, was very smooth, but he was stubborn from the time he started moving in my womb. Five days after he was born, he was turning himself in bed, and it was scary. He is very bubbly and my main challenge with him was that we went to the hospital a lot. In the first months, he had bracketed legs and a super sensitive skin. He looks like his father but his character and personality is so much like mine. He's basically a mini version of myself. Parenting two boys who are of extremely different personalities is such a learning experience. I have to constantly remind myself of their differences and how to handle them.

Raising them as a single mother too has also presented challenges. I will one day write a book about that too but overall, there is nothing that beats parenting with God and sound judgement.

Grieving each time

Given our culture that promotes resilience and strength, we tend to encourage people to "kwihangana", or be forbearing. I support the pursuit of patience and perseverance as values, and I also support resilience. On the flipside of this beautiful coin however, is the experience of pain and failure as a path to betterment.

When Mama died, I never fully grieved; never fully let out that scream of anguish, and allowed my heart to feel her loss. I had to persevere through that moment, and rightfully so. With time however, I came to understand that one has to find a way to grieve, let that pain out and find healing, or else it will find its own way out, and it's never pretty when the latter happens.

Such was my case. The next time I conceived, the pain of losing my mother came alive. The next time I pushed my son, the loss of her became real again. On random days with my children, I would feel her absence, and it always pained me that she would never get to see any of her grandchildren on this side of heaven.

The good thing is that I've learned to live with the remembrance of who she was by focusing on all the best that she gave us while she was still alive. Mama was cool, affectionate and loving, and those are some of the major parts of her character that I miss the most. Although it gets hard to remember her on some days, the beautiful memories always inspire and encourage me to give my children my best, making her loss more bearable. When I love and show them affection and tenderness as she did to us, I feel that I'm doing what she would have wanted me to do.

Raising great men

I have been blessed to mother two amazing boys; Koen and Keshawn, born five years apart, so different in character and nature, but so similar as brothers.

These children have taught me what the unconditional love of a mother looks like. It is a kind of love that makes me feel like my heart beats in my children's chests when I look at them. It is surreal. I experience it to this day, from the days I conceived them. Even more amazing is the fact that they love me back for being their mother.

When it comes to raising them, seeing that I have boys, and knowing well that I disagree with what our patriarchal societies have taught young boys to believe about manhood, I made it a point to raise them with the mindset of honoring women and not ever thinking that some roles were confined to women alone.

I teach my son, Koen, to do household chores that in another context would be done by the girl child. I want him to know how to wash dishes, cook, clean, clear the table, respectfully talk to me, or any other woman for that matter, and always know that he is not more special than the girl child just because he is a boy. With this mindset, I hope that he will grow up to be an outstanding son, father and husband. At the moment I write this book, the younger son is still a toddler, wreaking havoc in the house, but rest assured that he too will take his lessons soon.

I was raised Rwandan, to speak Ikinyarwanda, and to love my country. Against this backdrop, I was and still am determined to raise my children Rwandan as well. We speak Ikinyarwanda at home, and both boys take "guhamiriza" cultural dance classes.

Our culture contributes to who we are as a people and as parents, proud of who we are and raising the next generation of Rwandans who will stand on the shoulders of the greatness that we have experienced in our generation, it is paramount that we teach our young ones from an early age who they are as Rwandans. This can take on various forms but as long as we are committed to it, our children will benefit a lot from the knowledge of their identity and the values that our beloved country is built upon.

Enjoying the blessing of motherhood with Koen R.H on my left and Keshawn R.H on my right

No more control

I have an insecurity that comes from my fear of being terrible at motherhood. Back in the day, I had control over so many things, and that stimulated a mindset of perfection in me. I like to know what's coming, and prepare myself early on. As such, I lose my mind when there's no consistency. I'm one to have a number of Plan Bs for whatever I do.

I can't function without structure, and without it, I feel like I'm dying. I don't like surprises and unpredictability, because they cause me anxiety.

Imagine what it was like then, having stubborn sons who have pillow fights, break and spill stuff around the house. I was painfully stripped of my perfectionist agenda, and I had no choice but to tone down. I had to adjust to sharing my space with my two boys, and to raise them without expecting perfection from them.

I had to create more room for the unexpected, and let go of some control. That took a lot of faith; faith in God and His grace to mother these boys. I constantly remind myself that things will not always go my way. With all the unpredictable events I experienced throughout my life, God has taught me how to trust in Him and this has often meant one thing: letting go.

Motherhood has stretched me. The first few months after a newborn arrives have done a lot in teaching me not to live for myself. Gone was the beautiful sleep, the warm bed sheets, stretching in bed and enjoying the serenity of rest, in came the worry for my babies, the constant dreaming of who they should become in society, the anxiety and fear of getting it wrong and spending the rest of my life regretting that I must have damaged them in any way and the constant efforts to be a better mother. Motherhood? Motherhood is a gift yet a burden. A life lived for those humans that we birth. I am forever grateful for the gift while cognizant to the fact that these blessings come with a cost. The cost of loving another human being who feels like an extension of your heart and soul...and this feeling never stops. But again, a tremendous blessing that so many pray and weep to God for and never get their prayers answered.

For those who have been blessed in this manner, the greatest service that parents can render to their families, communities, churches and nations is to raise their children to be good people, respectful, kind and responsible. Nothing trumps a good upbringing, full of values, and a purpose driven life.

A child who has been given enough love and attention, and taught the necessary fundamentals, will grow up to be a solution in society, and not a problem. With these statements, I am not ignorant of the extraneous circumstances with which many of us have grown up in. I am simply saying that our generation of young parents can do better, and if we put our minds to it, we will do it.

We owe it to our children.

Chapter Twelve

Shaped By Hustle

In 2014, I graduated with a bachelor's degree in Mass Media and Communications from Mount Kenya University. I was working at Authentic Radio at the time, and I began thinking about what more I could do with my God given gifts.

One evening, my husband asked me what I wanted to do with my life, and I remember telling him that I wanted to have a communications business and eventually host a talk show, but all of those things were still hazy in my mind. I didn't know how to start. The only thing that I knew for sure was that God had blessed me with the gift of communication and I simply had to work on acquiring the skills needed to move forward.

Also, there was a certain level that we wanted for our family to develop towards, and the salary I earned from the church wasn't cutting it. Since I had already served full time in ministry for ten years, I prayed to God and told Him; "God, I have given you my youth wholeheartedly. We have reached a point where our family wants to grow more but not on our current resources. Can you please release me to go and explore other possibilities?"

At the time, I had just given birth to my second child and I felt that I had to do more. I needed to find more ways to support my husband in providing for the family. My dreams were around self-employment or working for the UN as my father always wished for me.

I wanted something that could cross the borders of Rwanda. At the time, I also felt like there were a lot of opportunities to grab, if only I could find ways to position myself strategically.

At the beginning of 2018, after much prayer and soul searching, I felt a peace about leaving full time ministry and in February 2018, I decided to approach Apostle Gitwaza and told him that I was quitting. He asked me why and I told him that the church didn't have the money I wanted to be paid. Plain and simple. In an attempt to get me to stay, he asked how much I would want to get paid, and I unashamedly asked for a seven figure salary that I wanted, to which he said that it wouldn't be easy right then. This didn't surprise me because I knew how the church operated and the burdens it carried.

He asked what was next and I told him about my dreams for opening a communication company. He understood me and requested for me to stay a little longer so that there could be a smooth transition at Authentic Radio and TV. I had grown and learned so much there, and I assured him that I would always be available when needed, except when I had work engagements.

He couldn't believe that I was leaving, nonetheless, he prayed for blessings over my future endeavors.

Éclat Communications Ltd

After giving birth to my second born in 2017, I finally decided that I was going to open my own communications company. I figured that, if I used my skills to offer the same services to my clients, except this time around, generate increased income, we would benefit much.

Now, finding a name for my company was tiresome. Being a perfectionist, I went back and forth on names until I stumbled upon ÉCLAT COMMUNICATIONS with the help of Maxime Niyomwungeri, a friend who's a graphic designer. ÉCLAT (Glow) came from the French Word, "éclairer," which means to shed light or to enlighten. My vision and goal were centred on shedding light on communications by providing professional interpretation, translation, creative content production services and corporate communication services.

Maxime helped with the design of the company logo and off we went. Once everything was set and I had determined what I wanted to do with the company, I registered it. I can never forget the excitement that I had when I received my company registration copy on my email. I knew that there were many discoveries, successes and failures on the way, but I was committed.

After opening my company, I spent every working moment in the office thinking about how to grow the company, who to connect with and what to do. There were a lot of business opportunities in event planning, but the industry full of experienced sharks, made landing a contract very difficult.

I soon realised that even though the company wasn't generating income, I had to make money for myself as I sought growth opportunities.

I approached someone who has a foot in the industry and told them about my company and what I sought to do. I requested them for subcontracted gigs just for me to get by. That was very naive of me.

Getting an appointment with this person in itself wasn't easy, and all I wanted from them was the chance to interpret professionally and at least earn a monthly income. But, they never reached out at all, except for one time through their assistant, and only because the client specifically asked for me.

The day that I met them, I left their office feeling inferior and wondering how I was ever going to maneuver my way around these walls that I was discovering. I left knowing that I wouldn't get called back but I vowed that I would put in work on my end and one day, I would prove that I was worth supporting and encouraging.

There is no bad blood between us but taking that rejection was hard, until I reminded myself that all roads led to Rome.

A few weeks later, I decided to call one of my colleagues and friend, Clement J. Ndayishimiye. I told him that I had quit my job and I was ready to do full time interpretation. He was thrilled by the news of my availability and he immediately looped me in a number of projects that he was working on. For all the time that I worked with him in his own company, he offered me the opportunity to grow and hone my skills.

Around that same time, Éclat Communications landed a contract to work on a communication strategy of an international non-profit organization in Rwanda and with these small yet sure baby steps, I began to see that we were definitely going to get somewhere one day. Each single day, I always told myself; "Barbara, Rome wasn't built in a day and slowly by slowly, you will get there."

Even though Clement tremendously blessed my life when Éclat was just starting, I still wasn't able to get as much from it as I hoped I could, and

Redwoods Leadership: On my right; Shiphrah Kenganzi Kiiza and on my left, Hassan Kibirango

to make matters worse, COVID-19 hit the world by storm. But, as badly affected as the events industry was, God still took care of me and opened other doors.

Redwoods Leadership

One day I received a call from a good friend of mine, Hassan Kibirango. We have been friends for a while. Hassan was and still is one of those people who always encouraged and motivated me. On this call, he told me that I was going to get a call from a lady who was opening a company called Redwoods Leadership and needed someone to help with training and facilitation. I remember telling him; "Hassan, I have never trained people before, how will I make this?" to which he responded; "Are you willing to learn how to do it?" And I quickly told him; "Of course I am very willing to learn!"

Soon enough, Shiphrah Kenganzi Kiiza called me. We met at a coffee shop and connected right away as she described what she was working on and how she wanted me to consider joining her as a mentee. Soon enough, I was recruited as a "Redwood."

Redwoods Leadership leveled my communications skills and sharpened my facilitation skills such that I even benefited much more as an MC from these trainings. Alongside these two great souls that are Hassan and Shiphrah, I have been privileged to serve the Rwandan corporate world in ways that I never thought I could. These two taught me the priceless value that comes from being humble enough to accept to be coached and mentored. I could write a book about these two, but you get the point of what I mean.

In this life, all we need is a helping hand, someone to trust, teach and take you to the next level and these two just did exactly that.

The Barbara Show

In 2018, I was slowly building up towards consistent content production. In doing so, I was also looking for other available opportunities in moderating events. I also observed that Rwanda didn't have many renowned MCs and when there were big events, those from Uganda and Kenya were the ones often flown in to do the job. I couldn't see many of us locals doing it often or on a large scale like these other consulting MCs.

Being one to love a challenge, I set my eyes on that too. I didn't need to start with an international event, all I needed was one local opportunity. I was determined to make my clients satisfied, as hard as it was to get such jobs.

Dear reader, getting my foot in the door wasn't easy, even though I brought other skills as a multilingual interpreter and journalist by profession. I constantly wondered how I was ever going to get skilled or even hired as a professional MC.

Noting that I was struggling to get people to actually see my skills and offer me opportunities, I took a different route. I started thinking of content creation; hosting a TV show to be more specific. In my mind, I reasoned that If I could create a product that could impact the society but also showcase my capacities, this product could be used to open the doors for me. With my background in media and passion for social transformation, I had always wanted to do a show, but it had never materialized.

I shared this idea with a few friends and they loved it, saying that it would showcase my skills and it would be the perfect way to account for my capabilities as a moderator.

Now, I knew what to do but knowing how and where to start this, it was still unclear. One day, I gave a ride to one of my friends, Alex Ntare. I told him about my idea to start a TV show and that I didn't know how to start. It turned out that he had a venue in which I could set up and host the show. We agreed with Alex that I would get a room, decorate it and get ready to start tapings for the show. After a few months, I managed to get some funds and began to decorate the room that I would use for the show.

Unfortunately, sooner than expected, the owners of the compound wanted their premises back and we all had to move out just as I had finished my setup. That was a major setback for me. I remember going silent on this dream for like one whole year. I looked at the time and money that had just been wasted, and felt like I didn't have it in me to start again and invest afresh. In addition, I didn't have the money to do so again. So, I shelved the whole idea.

In 2020, a former work colleague from Authentic Radio & TV, Jean de Dieu Kabanda opened a TV station called Isibo TV and offered me a slot on it. He showed me how he was willing to grow with me and would make the beginning easy so long as I committed myself to actually start the show. Soon after, I consulted with my friend, Rugasaguhunga (Rugasa) Ruzindana on going back in the arena of show production for mainstream media. He advised me to go for it but in all, pursue excellence.

After multiple consultations with Rugasa, I decided to try again. I got a friend from church who was in interior design; Claude Ndayisaba, to help me out with décor and Rugasa connected me with someone who would be tremendously instrumental in the success of the show. I was introduced to Mazimpaka Jean Pierre (JP), a multimedia producer and owner of ViFo Images. JP bought into my dream and we kicked it off in October 2020.

Calling the show; The Barbara Show came after consulting with a trusted friend who specialized in communications and we both agreed that this was a catchy and easy to remember name.

The first episodes were shot in Gikondo, a suburb in Kigali, at the Isibo TV studios for 2 hours and from then, I knew the system to use to get this baby moving.

As I edit this book, the show is now over one year old. I am happy and so proud of myself. So proud that I didn't let the fear of failure chain me to inaction.

Rwanda Leaders Fellowship

I got connected to the Rwanda Leaders Fellowship by my friend, Moses Ndahiro. It's an organization that, since 1995, seeks to instill Godly values in leadership. They host events like The National Prayer Breakfast and Young Leaders Conference. Its founding members are Ambassador Murigande Charles, Rev. Dr. Rutayisire Antoine and Rudahunga Gedeon.

In 2014, this organization involved more youths from different churches, institutions and businesses in their events. From the moment that we took part in these events, we knew that we belonged.

RLF leadership took us on board as new members and right away began to mentor us. It was also during these Prayer Breakfast events that I had the honor to officially host (MC) such national events that were broadcasted on the state's media platforms.

When I reminisce on my journey in the RLF, the 2013 National Prayer Breakfast will always be a major highlight for me.

Professor Vincent Anigbogu, a renowned advocate for leadership transformation in Africa, had been invited as the guest speaker at the national prayer breakfast of that year and I was to interpret for him. More so, the President of the Republic of Rwanda, H.E. Paul Kagame would attend.

I remember attending the event with all my nerves at their peak. At the time, I didn't even know how to address all the powerful men and women. I remember sitting on the table that I had been assigned to with my then husband and trying to memorize how to address the top five leaders as well as the other leaders who were in attendance. I was so nervous! So nervous.

I was low key having a mini mental breakdown in my head. I couldn't get over the fact that I was speaking in front of the President of the Republic himself.

To make it even worse, twenty minutes into the sermon, Professor Vincent went on about righteousness, and I kept translating it as "Gukiranuka (Justice)" as it's written in the Kinyarwanda Bible, but it was the wrong word to use in that context.

Let me tell you what happened and I am sure that you will feel for me; the President whispered to one of the people who were seated with him at the high table to note down a word to correct. I remember seeing Mrs. Adélaïde Rudahunga coming towards us at the podium with a note in her hands. On the note was written "Ubutungane (Integrity)," which was the contextually correct word to use for that audience as well as everyone who was following on the state media platforms. She then whispered; "Barbara, His Excellency has requested that you use that word because it is more fitting in this context than the one you were using."

I almost dropped the microphone and bolted. The fact that he was actually listening to and correcting me almost fried my mind senseless. In my mind, I started doing what I do best; talk to myself, freak out, pray and do it all over again; "Barbara, you've got this. No I don't gat this! God, help me get this!"

Professor Vincent finally concluded his sermon and we went back to our seats. Everyone congratulated me and told me I was awesome but being the perfectionist that I am, I kept thinking; "Really? How?". A few minutes later, while deep in thought; a Republican guard approached me and whispered in my ear, telling me that the President wanted to talk to me.

I had been summoned and it all felt like a movie! My then husband encouraged me to stand and go towards where the President was sitting; at the front. The whole room turned to me, wondering what I had done for the President to call me. I felt like I was about to have a heart attack.

When I reached by his side, he spoke lightly that he wanted to give his speech in Kinyarwanda but didn't want to leave out the guest because of the language barrier. He then asked me to sit in his chair and interpret for the guest while he spoke. Though I did as I was told, my nerves convinced me that the world was ending. I couldn't believe that I was invited to sit in the chair of our Rwandan legend, let alone use my gift and talent to serve him and his guest. Saying it was an honour to serve and interact with him is an understatement and I will forever cherish that moment.

Being part of the Rwandan Leaders Fellowship broadened my view on patriotism, and I fell more in love with the different aspects of our nation; the church, government and private sectors. The organization sows seeds in the leadership of the nation, and investing in the future like that is what still makes me a part of it today. It gives me a sense of purpose, of doing something of value, and feeling that my thoughts and actions have contributed to such a worthwhile cause is very humbling.

Sitting next to Prof. Vincent Anigbogu in the 2013 National Prayer Breakfast at the Serena Hotel, Kigali.

Symposia Consult

The second highlight of my career getting into Symposia Consult, one of Rwanda's leading events management companies. Rumongi Aimable, the founder, is an impeccable interpreter with high standards when it comes to hiring people who work for him. In 2019, I received a call from Symposia Consult and was asked to work in that year's National Dialogue Council (Umushyikirano). This was at the time when I was going through my divorce, and my mind was all over the place. The opportunity couldn't have come at a worse time than that! I got up anyway and did what I had to do, despite the immense pressure that came with the nature of that event and the fact that the President's office staff would be listening in on the interpretation through headsets.

Working for Symposia Consult was validation and working in such a big Government event was the seal of that validation for me as a professional interpreter.

In the booth, I met up with a colleague, who congratulated me for coming this far and gave me a heads up that I had to bring my A+ game. Apparently, Rumongi had attended the event too and he had a habit of monitoring his interpreters by listening in whilst simultaneously focusing on the actual event itself. The colleague also told me that if I didn't perform to Rumongi's standards, I wouldn't ever be called again. Talk about added pressure.

I still managed to sit down and do my job as best I could, and trust me when I say that it wasn't easy. I was struggling with not focusing on my family issues and at the same time I was trying to remain focused on the event.

As we went for a tea break, I saw Rumongi walk towards me, and I immediately thought, "He's coming to dismiss me." To my surprise, he said as soon as he approached me, he said; "That was amazing. Why haven't you worked with me before? Expect a call from us whenever we have work."

To this day, he has delivered on his promise and I've worked on a number of events with them, including the renowned Paul Rusesabagina hearing that took place in March 2021, which was followed online by a number of nonprofit organizations and the international community.

Through my work with Symposia Consult, as an Interpreter, I feel like If I was to pursue a career, strictly in this world of interpretation, I would have the right set of professional skills because of the mentorship that I have received from different colleagues in this journey.

Peace Through Business

Peace Through Business is a business training program founded by Dr. Terry Neese through her Institute for Economic Empowerment of Women (IEEW) for women entrepreneurs. In 2019, I heard about it through a friend from church, who recommended it and sent me a link to apply. I applied and got in right away. Peace Through Business, through workshops, equips women in Rwanda and Afghanistan with the skills they need to run a thriving business.

I was taught by Chantal Munanayire, an incredible business woman who has mentored me through my entrepreneurial journey. She taught me to never give up in business. Her mantra, which I have espoused is; "Pursue your cloud until you reach your promised land".

The course made me fall in love with business and offered me the hope of one day becoming self-sufficient and financially independent as woman.

After three months, I completed the course and then traveled to the United States of America for the two weeks Leadership Development training for the 2019 graduating class. In this program, I awarded the NATIONAL BUSINESS ASSOCIATION SCHOLARSHIP AWARD.

Upon completing my class, I volunteered and gave back by empowering other women who took the training in 2020. I had been mentored and empowered to become what I was and I found it a privilege to do the same for other women.

From that experience, I learned the value of empowering women and women-owned businesses. It's no wonder that I ended up teaming up with a friend's wife in starting another business.

Lacia Scented Candles

I got introduced to Henry Kato by Obed Sean Musabe. I was introduced to Obed by my friends; Pastors Floribert and Alice Nzabakira. Obed Sean; as I call him; is my business advisor and I had worked with him on a number of projects before he introduced Henry to me. Henry and Obed were friends and they had this idea of making scented candles that they were working on. One day, Henry, Obed and Christelle Bamureke; Henry's wife with their son Kayongo Beldan met me at the Elevate Suites Hotel in Nyarutarama with samples of these candles that Christelle had homemade. They wanted my feedback on these samples and if possible, a partnership in this new business venture.

The candles had a strong refreshing scent; yet they were still their first trial production, especially the GO-LEMON. This was a good business opportunity; one that; if it took off; we would eventually do well in Kigali and beyond. I decided to get on board and partner with Christelle on this venture. Her expertise was in production and mine was in communication. We worked out the basics and decided to open a company as soon as possible.

We decided to call the company Lacia Creative Ltd. LACIA, a combination of both our mothers' names; LAURETTE and ANNONCIATA. Christelle and I founded this company, not just for business but as a testament of the legacy and pride that we held for both being our mothers' daughters.

This product has grown to have other types of candles which have filled our homes with fresh scents.

The UN

Of all my achievements as a person, nothing has ever made my father proud as me getting a job at the UN - International Residual Mechanism for Criminal Tribunals. In the year 2020, when the world was at a standstill because of the Coronavirus pandemic, everything froze and businesses shut down. I needed a regular and steady income generating business or a job to make it, given that my business which thrived on events and businesses open was struggling like all the others.

With single motherhood on the horizon, I definitely needed a reliable and consistent source of revenue. It was hard until an acquaintance of mine shared with me a link for a language assistant post in the UN IRMCT - Kigali office.

I applied for the job and fulfilled all the requirements but unfortunately wasn't taken on board from when I first applied. It was disappointing because I counted on the stability of that job but I didn't let it get in my head. I knew that God would take care of me and I just had to keep trusting Him. It wasn't until April 2021, when my divorce was finalised that I received an email from the UN, appointing me for the same job.

I was excited that I got such an opportunity but what I loved most, besides the financial stability and every other benefit that come with this job, is the fact that I have finally made my father happy. It now all makes sense and it was worth it.

Never would I have ever thought or even dreamt of becoming an entrepreneur. It just seemed so complex and very demanding that I believed that only men could pull it off. I guess I got that mindset from being raised by parents who held white collar jobs. Predictable, safe and comfortable. Entrepreneurship on the other hand, I have discovered is an exhilarating ride. The highs are HIGHS, the lows are LOWS and everything in between prepares you for the next wave of emotions. You have to keep coming for "it" until you find "it" or else, you will lose heart at dawn. I fell in love with the hustle simply because it taught me many lessons; negotiating, networking and the art of turning "NO" into a "YES".

Oh, and the little beginnings are something to behold! And no, do not get me wrong, I am not glossing over the fact that despite all my endeavors, there were times that I would spend months without work and was flat broke. Not giving up allowed me to reach to the next finishing line. Yes, entrepreneurship feels like there is always a new finishing line and once you are there, you come back and start again.

The hustle also taught me some of the greatest lessons in life; "Your network is your net worth" and "A good reputation is currency in business." I cannot even begin to imagine who and where I would be if I wasn't helped by the many people that I have encountered on this journey. I am most certain that if I hadn't worked on my reputation, it would be very difficult for me to enter some rooms today.

Dear reader, if you are in business, let me encourage you; the essential key is to keep the eyes on the ball. Do not give up just yet, who knows... tomorrow might offer you pleasant surprises.

Chapter Thirteen

Shaped By Friendship

Over the years, I came to realise that I'm an ambivert. Different people have met either the wild and crazy Barbara, or the calm one. Many of them are not more than acquaintances. Only a few have grown to become special friends of mine and have played different, recognizable roles in my life which have shaped me as a person.

They are the ones who have been with me through thick and thin, and stuck with me even when I walked down the dark alleys of my life, including my divorce. These are the people who are part of my everyday life, who make me feel good about myself, who make me laugh, who make me smile. These are the people who beautify my life and make it worth living. These are people, whose advices shape me each day.

Crazy Women

Crazy Women without being literally "crazy" is a group that consists of myself and three of my closest friends; Natasha Niyo Umutoni, Chouette Uwera Mwamikazi and Mary Umutoni Kanamugire.

Of all my friends, the longest closest friendship I have had is with Natasha. We've been close ever since we first met in 1998. We first met at Camp Kigali Primary School just after the Genocide Against the Tutsis. We grew up together, went to the same High Schools together and only momentarily separated when I went to live in London. Even then, we kept in touch on a regular basis that, when I came back home in 2007, it felt like we had just met the other day. Even in a long distance friendship, we navigated adolescence and grew up together. I remember us giving our lives to Christ around the same time and even serving in the same ministry together.

She is the first person who pushed me to prioritise my mental health and there's no way I could have gone through my huge pile of trauma and still function like a normal person without her.

She helped me see that I needed to love myself enough to get some help. As I struggled with my divorce, she was never judgmental, and she stuck with me all the way even on days that I made some very questionable decisions. God knew I needed that, more than I perceived and he gave me Natacha, for a filter free, safe and authentic sisterhood.

Chouette, I met in 2002 at Lycée de Kigali, my former high school. She was a class ahead of me. As a survivor of, and orphaned by the 1994 Genocide against the Tutsi, Chouette had been through so much, and I was drawn to her. I decided to love her into friendship and sisterhood.

Our friendship grew rapidly over the years. Even after she moved to Europe at some point, we always stayed in touch. When I was going to get married, she's one of the people who gave me the biggest financial contribution that helped sort out some urgent issues that me and my then fiancé were facing. Her contribution helped a lot and we couldn't believe she could go that far in supporting us. She is one of the few people that we have been through the different seasons of my life together. Strong, reliable, generous, trustworthy and loving are some of the adjectives that I can use to describe her.

Chouette taught me what empathy looks like, how to listen, how to understand and really feel for people suffering, loving them right and allowing them to also live in their truth.

She taught me selflessness and how to really be a good friend.

Mary and I found ourselves becoming neighbors in Bibare; Remera, Kigali in 1999. Our family had just moved from Kicukiro to Remera near where her family lived. We had friends in common but we also experienced our teenage years together as young girls living in the same neighborhood. At the time, we were both giving our lives to Christ and were so hungry for God. Our friendship was solidified by that hunger from the onset.

Our friendship deepened when I returned back home from the UK. She helped me re-adjust to life in Rwanda. A lot had changed and she helped with my transition.

She and Natacha really helped me in those first years back. When it was time to get married; they both singlehandedly planned for my wedding from the Gusaba (Dowry) ceremonies to the Gutwikurura (Unveiling of a bride). When I got pregnant with my first born son, she often went with me to the doctors' appointments and when I had Koen, she literally spent every single day at our home, doing what my mother, had she been alive, would have done.

Mary showed me that one doesn't need to be of a certain age to be someone else's anchor.

Reunion

My second circle of friends is Reunion, a group of friends that I went to high school with. We meet once or twice a year but thanks to technology, we are always connected to each other besides those few moments that we meet in a year.

We all come from different backgrounds, mindsets, and even religions, but I love how our dynamic works in spite of all that. Reunion is simply people being people without any biases and whenever we have a reunion, we allow ourselves to enjoy our youth without the duties and responsibilities that have come with our age.

Abou Baker Mulangwa, whom I call Papa Bear, is a Hajj and it's refreshing to see that we are bonded despite our varying beliefs. He's one of the kindest people I know; serious to a fault yet so endearing if you get to know him.

Over the years, Abou has taught me how to tap into relationships and opportunities irrespective of different opinions and backgrounds.

Dr. Felix Rutaganda has a sense of humour that very few can understand. He is a kind and hardworking guy. Felix is one the few classmates turned to friends that are still present in my life. A doctor turned to hustler; his relentless pursuit of business growth is so commendable.

Victor Rukundo is the hustler who sells anything that human beings need on a daily basis. Whatever you need, best believe he has it. He's not one to say much, but he's one person to rely on any given day.

Both Felix and Victor are small business owners who inspire me each day.

Nadia Nyamuniga is the chef of the group, the disciplinarian and many other things that I cannot dare describe here; of course for my own personal security. I know these statements alone will get me into trouble with Mrs. Ruzindana. She's the boss lady who puts us all in our place and calls a spade a spade…no filter. She's a breath of fresh air. Nadia surprised a lot me during the season of my divorce. She was so concerned and always called to check on me. She would take me out often, just to show me that I wasn't alone in this. She's a wonderful soul. An intelligent woman, very driven and a go – getter, Nadia shapes me in the sense that she has shown me that motherhood isn't an excuse to use as one abandons their dreams.

Zainab Kibibi is that girlfriend that you'll laugh with about everything and nothing. She is such a sweetheart. Along with Nadia, she is one of the most stylish people I know. Zainab is thoughtful and very caring. Zainab has taught me the true definition of selflove and looking out for all that is positive and healthy. We both have this saying, "We do not want any wahala (trouble)" and this raises a certain intentionality on guarding our peace.

If I was to share here what and who she has been in my life, I'm pretty sure the WhatsApp group would have her on a platter! He he he he he!

Oscar Mucyo is humble, talented and very smart. Oscar is that good friend that you look at and wonder; from which rock did I crawl from. Very well raised, kind to a fault and not judgmental, Oscar is that friend who always shows me that pursuing growth and living authentically is what this whole journey called life should be about.

Natacha who got her first mention in another chapter in this book, is also part of this group but since it might seem like she is taking over the whole dance floor, she won't get more than two sentences here, actually three or four sentences. I can tell you that as she reads this part, she is rolling her eyes at me. I can always tell when she does that to spite me but it's all good.

Lastly, Gael Rutembesa, who helped me write this book, is an amazing human. He's the brother that I always felt like I could share the "tea" with. Working with him on this book project brought us close and taught me a lot about the art of listening.

What makes these friends of mine special is that they don't treat me as a, "Pastor" and they don't put me on a pedestal. They don't have holier than thou expectations of me and there's no pressure for me to be perfect or always say the right thing every time. I love how they celebrate and also make fun of my accomplishments. I love that they allow me to be me. Such is the friendship that has shaped me to live my life unapologetically authentic.

CCC Storytellers

This group started as a professional WhatsApp group, with people working in the Communications field who came together to help our friends who are survivors of the Genocide against the Tutsi and who had published books. Charles Habonimana, Pierre Claver Irakoze and Celine Uwineza were the reason we all got together but with Pamela Mudakikwa, Rugasaguhunga Ruzindana and I, we decided to be more than just a Whatsapp group. We became friends. This group has simply made me fall in love more, fully respect and honor Genocide survivors. They have taught me what it means to live, to love and lead a successful life despite the traumas of our past.

Charles or Karoli as we love to call him is someone that I consider as a brother. He had a sister who would be my age today but was killed in the Genocide against the Tutsis.

One day, after the 2019 commemoration of Genocide against the Tutsis, we went together to Mayunzwe where he showed me where he was born and where he grew up. When I told him my age, there, in Mayunzwe, he looked at me and told me that I was officially adopted in his family because I reminded him of his sister. His resilience shaped my view on survival and always inspires me.

Celine is in the same age bracket as I, and I see so much of myself in her. She is a strong, resilient woman with so much empathy and so much soul. Her love for keeping a low profile will not allow me to on in details about all that we have shared over the years but I have always loved "flexing" as her friend. A businesswoman in her own right, Celine, in my book, is the definition of "Beauty and Brains".

Claver, I met through the rest of the group members with whom I already forged special friendships, and I wasn't going to let him be the exception. He is emotionally intelligent and very understanding. We became close friends after the day that he told me that we couldn't be friends without our families meeting and bonding. For him, it was either that or nothing, and I became a family friend like that. Our children have grown to become friends, him and his wife are wonderful people that I consider family friends.

Pamela and I go way back. I met Pamela before connecting in this group. We met in 2017 for the first time and decided that we had to be friends. Very intelligent and caring to a fault. We have been through so much together, survived so many storms and we both know that we are here, and better people because of what we went through.

Rugasaguhunga Ruzindana is that discipline prefect in High School who was unrelenting in getting us organised, for our benefit of course. One thing I have learned about him is to pursue my dreams and never stop until I get to where I want to get. Rugasa is the man who has dared me to pursue success for each single dream of mine. Not to just dream but to actually do and after doing, pursue success. He is my drawing board and this book wouldn't even be in your hands if hadn't read its first written chapter and told me to keep writing.

Other Friends

I have a few close friends from church. Pastor Christian Ibambasi is one of them. We got close in 2015 and he's one of the coolest men I have ever met. There is a lot that I didn't understand about life because of the naivety and immaturity that I had but he taught me so much. I first worked closely with Christian when we were organizing Authentic Tours to Israel. He is a pro when it comes to logistics. He provided the support that our office needed from organizing here in Kigali to actually operating the tour in Israel. Working with him gave me a lot of boldness and courage to take charge and face challenges. We then became friends from that time.

Christian literally took me in as the big brother I never had but always needed. He always and still does look out for me, you would think I am his last born sister. We have walked through some dark nights together and we have both seen the hand of the Lord upon our lives. One of the reasons I have stayed friends with him is because he is a man of his word and he is not in the business of lip service. He is loyal and empathetic and his own life experience has served to sharpen my mind by teaching me some major key life lessons.

Christian and his wife Annie Tabura stood by me when I was going through so much pain brought by my divorce. When I think of them, I ask God; "What did I do to get so lucky and blessed to have such amazing people in my life?" This couple taught me the true meaning of *"Through thick and thin,"* when they chose to carry and love me through that dark time of my life, and for them, I will always be grateful.

Secondly, there's Clement Jules Ndayishimiye who took a chance on me and taught me how to do simultaneous interpretation in the booth. I didn't know much about booth work but he was willing to help nurture my talent professionally. He once told me that one day I might want to leave full time ministry and join the corporate world; then, I would need to have a skill that would serve as a cushion to fall on. By this statement, Clement offered me gigs over the years and this sustained me for a long time. He equipped me with the right skills to survive when that day to leave full time ministry came.

Clement created opportunities that shaped me into the professional interpreter that I am and for that, I'll forever be indebted.

Amongst others, there's Pastor Floribert Nzabakira, whom I worked with at Authentic Radio. I met Flori, as I like to fondly call him; at the church. At the time, he was working for RWANDATEL in Muhanga. We didn't grow close until when we found ourselves working together at the Radio. Flori had done extensive work in the Media and what I did not master in Broadcasting Media, he taught me.

Our connection and friendship served us well in that, together, we managed the Radio and also hosted a morning talk show every day; ***"Life Today."*** Beyond that, we went on to do various Communication projects together in the church which honed my communication skills.

Our friendship carried us through quite a number of hurdles in our work and we both managed to grow and learn so much from each other in that season.

I first met Muteteri Eugenie when I had first started working at the church; back in 2008. We were age mates, both young and in full time ministry. Both of us didn't really get the sense of our service in church at such a young age; nonetheless, we both were convinced more than anything that God wanted us at the church for that particular season. While I worked in the Administration of the church, she was a full time intercessor and evangelist.

On a social note, we also had Mary as a mutual friend. Muteteri as an intercessor and a Pastor prayed with me and for me for a long time. Her commitment and loyalty to our friendship shaped me in the sense that it kept me hopeful for better days ahead. We have been great friends for all these years.

He requested me to keep his name anonymous but I jokingly call him my chief advisor, oh well, depending on the joke of the day, I have a nickname for him. The first of many times that we shared lunch; this friend connected to my soul as a lifelong friend would do.

From then on, we became inseparable. We always joke that we are each other's teachers in languages; Kinyarwanda for him and English for me, but we teach each other more about life than anything else.

When I was going through my divorce, he told me one thing; "You will never walk alone. You might be at fault in your struggles but that does not warrant any form of rejection. I will make sure that I stay." And he did!

There were times that I was so hopeless and never believed that there would ever be a day where I would laugh from within or enjoy life, and in those those times; he would tell me me; "Rust does not change the fact that a metal is a metal. Your divorce should never define you." With him, I always knew that I would rise from the ashes like a phoenix.

Chantal Munanayire is one of the few women that I have met who have managed to be successful and still remain humble and kind.

She and I started with a facilitator/student relationship when she was teaching me alongside my fellow trainees in the Peace Through Business 2019 cohort. We eventually evolved our professional relationship to sisterhood.

I remember starting my business and taking the PTB program to generally understand how a business ran to actually falling in love with the hustle because of this woman! She taught us with so much ease and confidence yet with such humility that she always left us wanting more. On so many occasions, she would tell me, "Barbara, follow your cloud." Derived from a Bible verse in the book of Exodus, which states "Follow your God to where He is leading you."

Chantal's sisterhood shaped me to become the entrepreneur that I am today and she is that big sister that I know I can always count on.

Family will always be family but there are some family members who prove to be more than family but friends. Lifelong friends. Such is Richard Nduwarugira, my maternal cousin, Darlington T. Kabatende and Asiimwe John Ishabairu who are my paternal cousins. They have all played similar roles of empowerment in my life but in different ways. Richard and Darlington are the dotting friends, big brothers and constant life coaches who always remind me of my worth while Asiimwe is the cousin/friend who always seeks to ensure that I work on becoming the best version of myself. This trio has shaped me to become a better family member, always seeking for the betterment of my loved ones; and for this am grateful to them. Immensely.

Pamela Mutijima, more than a friend but a big sister, is one of the few friends that I call sisters simply because we have drunk from the same cup. Pamela once told me this; "May my own life experiences be the map that guides you as you navigate these unchartered waters of being called a divorced woman and a single mother. If I survived, you too will survive, and one day, you will help someone else survive these storms."

With this statement, I recognize the force that she has been in my life, before and after the dissolution of my marriage.

This far in business, I have learnt a few lessons here and there. I have been shaped by failures and success but nothing beats the "push" that only Obed Sean Musabe gives me.

I met Obed when I was persevering in business but the moment, I talked to him about what I dreamt of becoming as a business woman, the pressure was on. Obed taught me how to think on my feet, work fast and be consistent until I got results.

The latest lesson from him is pitching business ideas. My oh my! What an adrenaline rush this has given me! He squeezed me out of my comfort zone and showed me how to execute all my plans.

I always tell him that everyone needs a "Sean" in their life if they want to grow. Besides shaping me in business, he is a great friend, one that we never fail to laugh with, even when situations are intense. For him, I am very grateful to God for crossing our paths.

My list of friends would be incomplete if I failed to introduce to you, dear reader, a friend that I lost ten years ago.

Lidwine Niyonizeye and I connected when we were still in High School at La Colombière. We remained friends for the whole time that I was away in London and she in Algeria.

Eventually, she went to live in Canada and that's where she passed on, in 2012. Her loss broke my heart because Lidwine was one of the realest friends that I had.

We always joked that we would one day make a lot of money and retire early with our husbands and spend the rest of lives traveling the world, watching our husbands play golf while we went to spas to get pampered. We intended to live the "soft" life together in our old age, unfortunately, she passed on early.

I miss her a lot. I miss our long emails. I miss our long phone calls. I miss her.

May her memory be a blessing and may we never forget this great soul that passed on in her youth.

Isn't God amazing? That in each season of our lives, He prepares people who will hold our hand and show us the way? I couldn't have been a better person, had I not had the privilege of having great humans in my life as friends, adopted brothers and sisters.

When we are choosing friends, we have different criteria that we follow but it's not often that we ask ourselves, "How is this person impacting my life for the better? How am I impacting their life for the better? Is this a person worth keeping in my life? When push comes to shove, will this person remain in my life? Will I stand with them when all hell breaks loose?"

As the saying goes, *"Birds of a feather flock together,"* I pray that we find the right birds to flock together for they directly or indirectly shape us.

Lidwine Niyonizeye, Algeria 2004. May you continue to rest easy sis. You will always be missed.

Conclusion

When I started out with this book, I didn't really think that it would get here. What started as a healing journal entry actually became the push to look deep within my soul and sift through my life experiences in search for God's healing and victory in my life.

SHAPED is not simply a written testimony of my life, SHAPED is a healing manuscript of my soul, the pen that gave me the courage to finally face my soul deep within and acquire the courage that I needed to tell myself my truth and share with you that same gift.

I hope that this gift offered will lead you to that same place, revisit some painful chapters of your life and find healing for yourself. You deserve it.

If anything, may this memoir help you to celebrate the shape that you have acquired from the different life experiences that you too have lived through because each experience counts.

May your life forever be SHAPED.